PRAISE FOR *TWO WORLDS AT WAR*

In my several years in ministry and nine years as International Missions Director of The Church of Pentecost, a global Pentecostal movement currently operating in 105 countries on six continents, I have observed the daily struggles brewed in the "boiling pot" of parent-child relationships in the diaspora. Such conflicts render many families unstable. The timeless principles and in-depth knowledge contained in this book, *Two Worlds at War,* put forth by Rev. Dr. and Dr. Portuphy, hold the keys to loosening these cultural and intergenerational cords. The book is borne out of deep conviction, extensive research, and firsthand personal experiences of this lovely couple. It is also a rich Christian resource that can assist ministers and counselors at all levels in their work, especially among the youth. The careful use of literary devices and the simplicity of writing makes for easy reading. It is one rare book you cannot put down until you are done reading it.

—APS. EMMANUEL GYASI ADDO
International Missions Director, The Church of
Pentecost, Worldwide

Christian immigrant families in the diaspora have long battled the wave of cultural tension in their homes. In *Two Worlds at War*, Rev. Dr. and Dr. Portuphy provide a practical and relevant approach to mending the broken walls resulting from this tension, using a research-based approach. The years of service that the authors have garnered in the youth ministry and ministry to the older first-generation immigrant parents have been brought to bear on every page of the book. I do highly recommend this book to every Christian immigrant family and seminaries that train ministers who serve multicultural congregations.

—APS. MICHAEL AGYEMANG-AMOAKO
National Head, The Church of Pentecost, U.S.A.

Mike and Cynthia are great parents from unique families. They have tremendous experience in family issues partnering in ministry. Their voices in this book *Two Worlds at War* is an embodiment of parents and children's episodes in the home. You will find yourself in it. Get a copy and be enriched and beyond.

—APS. DR. EMMANUEL A. OWUSU
National Head, The Church of Pentecost, Canada

In *Two Worlds at War,* the authors share biblical and practical insights for bridging the cultural divide between African immigrant parents and Western-born/raised children. Readers will find it therapeutic due to the common thread of hope that runs through the fabric of its chapters.

—APS. DR. MBAYANE, S. MHANGO
Principal, Pentecost Biblical Seminary

Anyone who has raised teenagers knows how challenging communication and culture can be between the generations. This is especially true for immigrant families and their children. In *Two Worlds at War,* Drs. George and Cynthia Portuphy have extensively studied the interaction between African immigrant parents and their children raised in the USA and provide viable methods for parents and their children to overcome their cultural differences. I highly recommend this book to parents, pastors, and leaders who are working with children and teenagers of immigrant families or anyone desiring practical tools to bridge the cultural gaps between youth and older generations.

—DR. BOB SAWVELLE

Founding and Senior Pastor of Passion Church Tucson, Arizona, Author, Adjunct Professor Global Awakening Theological Seminary

With several telling stories, *Two Worlds at War* spotlights the cultural, generational, and language gaps between parents and children in African immigrant families in the United States. It points to principal keys to a successful family life of immigrants when parents and children recognize the differences of each other by shifting their mindsets in Christ and by lowering their mutual expectations. The negotiating paradigm shift this book suggests may also significantly help immigrant families from Asia and Latin America. This excellent book is a must-read for immigrant parents, church pastors, and cross-cultural counselors, and public school teachers of the young.

—DR. ANDREW PARK

Professor of Theology and Ethics, United Theological Seminary, Dayton, OH

In *Two Worlds at War,* Pastor Dr. and Dr. Portuphy—marriage and ministry partners, seasoned youth workers, and immigrant parents to three American-born children—have provided an intercultural and intergenerational hermeneutic that can help immigrant parents and their Western-bred children to achieve harmoniously, God-honoring parent-child relationships.

Two Worlds at War will reveal such insights on cross-cultural and intergenerational differences to the extent that one read will not be enough!

—APS. DAVID NYANSAH HAYFRON
Former Youth Director, The Church of Pentecost, Ghana

Pastor Dr. Mike and Mrs. Dr. Cynthia Portuphy have eloquently addressed the common issues immigrant parents and their children face in the Western world. Such families may either adopt an attitude of "cultural correctness" or absolute "cultural integration." Either extreme is a false balance, which has negative consequences (Prov. 11:1). The insights they bring in this book will benefit every immigrant family as they maneuver their way through multiple cultures and generations. I highly recommend *Two Worlds at War* to pastors and youth leaders.

—APS. EBEN QUAYE
National Head, The Church of Pentecost, Germany, Regional
Coordinating Council Coordinator for Europe

This book, *Two Worlds at War,* holds a perfect and practical key to unlocking the closed cultural jackets that seem to divide our worlds, our homes, and our families. In this book, Rev. Dr., and Dr. Portuphy echo the idea that the approach immigrant parents must adopt towards their Western-born children is to *"Win their hearts before they break your heart."* Such parental style usually produces a reciprocal effect from children. I highly recommend the knowledge revealed in this book to all immigrant families to read and adopt in mitigating our families' cultural challenges.

—REV. BISMARK OSEI AKOMEAH
Author, General Overseer of one of the largest African Immigrant
Churches in the United States, Jesus Power Assembly of God, Ohio

Praise For Two Worlds At War

In *Two Worlds at War,* Rev. Dr. and Dr. Portuphy offer a workable solution to foster cohesion between the two worlds. This book resonates with my experience of working with the youth and parenting children born in the West. It shares clear insights through real-life experiences and teases out the challenges confronting both children born in the diaspora and their parents born and raised in a different culture. I recommend this book as a must-read to every parent and the youth.

—DIANA HAMILTON
Award-Winning Gospel Artist, Immigrant Parent, U.K.

Pastor Dr. George and Dr. Cynthia Portuphy narrate with simplicity, moving stories, rooted in qualitative research, ministry exposure, personal experience, and godly counsel the conflict that exists between immigrant parents and their children living in the West, and suggests ways of peaceful coexistence. In their eye-opening book, *Two Worlds at War,* both parents and young people will acquire a depth of wisdom in how to effectively relate to each other when they find themselves in conflicting cultures. I highly recommend it to everyone, especially those searching for ways to understand the youth and vice versa.

—REV. DR. BENJAMIN DEBRAH, Ph.D.
Pastor, The Church of Pentecost, UK, Immigrant Parent

This book is an excellent resource for advice to all immigrant parents from experienced educators, ministers, and immigrant parents, George and Cynthia Portuphy. I have spent many years with them and directly observing their children and members in their ministry, and I see that the authors model and demonstrate that immigrant families can overcome adversities and be successful in raising children who are ready to fulfill their God-given callings. This book can speak to people of any culture, bridging the gap between the generations.

—DR. SANG SUR, Th.D., Ph.D.
President, Prayer Tents, CEO, Sciturus Real Investment Group

Two Worlds at War is a hands-on exposé that explores the different worlds that immigrant parents and their children navigate in their adopted home country. It seeks to provide tools that both sides can utilize effectively to bridge that gap. The book is an invaluable tool, and dare I say, a must-read for parents looking to raise well-adjusted Christian children in the diaspora.

OREOLUWA UDOFIA, ESQ.
Assist. General Counsel, GoDaddy; Immigrant Parent

TWO WORLDS
AT WAR

*Finding Common Cultural Grounds
for African Immigrant Parents and
Their Children*

GEORGE M. PORTUPHY, DMIN,
AND CYNTHIA ADOM-PORTUPHY, PHD

XULON PRESS

Xulon Press
2301 Lucien Way #415
Maitland, FL 32751
407.339.4217
www.xulonpress.com

Paperback ISBN-13: 978-1-6322-1509-3

Hardcover ISBN-13: 978-1-6628-0321-5

Ebook ISBN-13: 978-1-6322-1510-9

To all immigrant families with multiple generations maneuvering their way through the nuances of their cultural differences to create heartfelt and thriving homes.

TABLE OF CONTENTS

ACKNOWLEDGMENTS

First and foremost, we would like to give all praise to our Lord and Savior, Jesus Christ, who birthed this message in the depths of our hearts and burdened us enough to pen down these precious nuggets on finding commonalities and grounds of understanding in two worlds that are at war—immigrant homes.

Our special thanks go to the Chairman of The Church of Pentecost Worldwide, Apostle Eric Kwabena Nyamekye, for his godly counsel and graciously writing the Foreword for this piece, despite his numerous responsibilities. We are indebted to the National Head of The Church of Pentecost, USA, Apostle Michael Agyemang-Amoako who truly urged us on to work on this project. We would also like to appreciate the International Missions Director, Apostle Emmanuel Gyasi Addo and the National Head of the Church of Pentecost Canada, Aps. Dr. Emmanuel Anthony Owusu for their fatherly support. To Apostles Samuel K. Arthur and Dr. John K. Appiah, we say thank you for your continuous counsel. Finally, we are grateful to the national executive council, USA for their fatherly oversight.

The parents and youth of The Church of Pentecost, Columbus district, Ohio and Virginia district, Virginia deserve a laudable commendation. You shared with us the realities of your struggles as you maneuver through your two worlds—this formed the backbone of our book. To Rev. Dr. Robert Baah, Mimi Brako Bismarck, and Jada Nyarko, we say thank you for your meticulous editorial support.

Special thanks to Xulon Publishers for a yeoman's job. Our first encounter with you encouraged us to push ourselves to get this on the shelves and into the hearts of so many people who need this message of hope. Thank you for making our dream become a print reality.

Finally, we are grateful to our three lovely children, Valerie, Verna, and Vince-Mike, who have allowed us to develop our parenting skills as first-generation immigrant parents. Our successes and mistakes in the process of raising you due to our cultural differences have birthed this book. Thank you for all your sacrifices. Thank you for your tolerance. Thank you for understanding that even though we may be worlds apart, we are the same.

FOREWORD

Perhaps part of the beauty of this book is that it is co-authored by a man and his wife, both of whom are well-educated and culturally observant. The authors write this book not just as researchers but as African parents who have raised their children in North American culture even though they grew up in Africa. Also, they have served as ministers, pastoring and counseling in traditional African churches and the youth, under The Church of Pentecost, in North America. Having lived in North America and adjusted to its culture and values, they are better qualified to discern the nuances of the two cultures.

Often, culture dictates our behaviors and attitudes. Besides, opinions and phrases differ from one culture to the other. For instance, what one considers disrespectful in a culture would not be so regarded in another. Such differences are exacerbated in immigrant homes in the Western world where the culture of immigrant parents and that of their Western-born or raised children may collide. In *Two Worlds at War*, the authors justifiably call this cultural tension a *war*.

We live in a digital postmodern world—a world with tenets that contradict traditional (African) moral values on parent-child relationships. In the Western world, the permissive and individualistic lifestyle, which props independence, empowers the youth to crave more autonomy. The challenge for the immigrant parent, (raised in a culture with restrictive, top-down, communalistic flavoring) in such cultures is raising their children in an environment that does not allow them to bring these children up to become *like them*.

Supported by research, the book serves a useful guide for all immigrant parents living in the diaspora, and for the youth, who, growing up, may not understand the real sources of tension at home. Thus, the authors not only highlight the challenges of parental training in immigrant households, but they also offer suggestions for the mutual winning of the war within immigrant families. These include the need for parents and children alike to acknowledge the different cultures and environments in which they live and attempt to adjust by dropping their respective *cultural weapons* and *iron cast mindsets* that engender tension in the family.

The authors write: "Immigrant families face two opposing worlds—worlds divided by generations and cultures. They must adjust not only to the intergenerational differences in a new environment, but also they have to negotiate between two cultural worlds: Western and African culture." The war doesn't just occur in homes but in the church as well. The issues involve the youth's desire for a relational religion in which the church manages to meet their deep emotional and spiritual needs. The authors expertly discuss this issue in the book.

The authors further encourage Christian youth to be *agents of change* wherever they may find themselves—high schools, college campuses, or the workplace. The youth should not reject the church because of cultural and generational conflicts. As they put it: "You may probably be the change agent God may use to transform the church." That certainly is good advice!

We live in a global village, where the internet makes information easily accessible—cultures and value systems in one part of the world get across to the other like a viral pandemic. Therefore, the discussions in this book are not for those in North America or the diaspora only. The lessons are handy for all parents and the youth and youth workers across the globe, because the lessons are transcultural.

Two Worlds at War is an easy-to-read book, spiced with imaginatively dramatized examples to prod the reader on. You must read it to find more for yourself. I recommend it unreservedly to you.

—APOSTLE ERIC NYAMEKYE
Chairman, The Church of Pentecost, Worldwide

INTRODUCTION

Sarah is a twenty-five-year old pharmacist. Her parents, a Christian African immigrant family, have lived in the United States for the past twenty-two years. At the age of eleven, she joined them in the United States. Sarah is shy, quiet, and reserved. However, beneath her seemingly calm demeanor lies a pile of abusive experiences and untold stories. At her age, she has not just suffered physical beatings and name calling but has endured four years of sexual abuse from the hands of her uncle while she was in Africa. She could not share this experience with anyone—it remained a hidden battle.

After joining her parents in the United States, Sarah hoped she could open up for the first time and share her story. However, after she arrived, she attempted on multiple occasions to do so, but on every single attempt, she hesitated because her mom was too quick to judge her. Sarah could not connect with her parents on a deeper level because they were physically absent when she was young. Eventually, she vowed never to disclose her experience to them because she reasoned, "If I have managed to deal with this issue at a very young age, then I might as well continue dealing with it alone—no one would understand me." Life went on, but the years of abuse left her emotionally traumatized. She felt used, unloved, and rejected.

Sarah immersed herself in the American educational system and the ways of living. Gradually, she started shedding her accent, her language, her clothing, and almost everything African. Within just two years, Sarah had fully immersed herself into the mainstream Western culture. Her parents began to complain about her taking on a culture that was too liberal. To them, that culture was anti-Christian. In the initial years, life was hard for her as she strove to adjust to the cultural change, maneuvering between the predominantly African culture at home, and the contrasting American culture at school. Sarah had to contend with defining her identity. In her middle school, she felt different among her peers—in a negative way. These experiences led to mild depression. She found solace in stress-eating and gained a lot of weight. Gradually, people changed how they labeled her. She was no longer the girl from Africa; she was the fat girl. Her parents did not make things any better for her as they kept beating her down for overeating.

At a point, Sarah realized that she was facing abuse again—just a different kind. She felt nobody cared about her feelings just like when she was in Africa. That hurt her so badly. From the age of fifteen, already feeling useless, she gave herself to any boy who considered her beautiful or who she thought at the least, understood her. She shared her abusive stories with these guys, thinking they could be trusted. But every encounter was short-lived, as they used and dumped her. This cycle continued for ten years! At the age of twenty-five, Sarah was tired. She could not trust anyone—family or friends. One summer, she decided to end it all. Sarah attempted suicide on three different occasions. Amazingly, all attempts failed. She still lived!

It was one quiet October night in 2014 at about 11:00 P.M. The lights were out, and we had retired to bed. An anonymous call came through. We picked up the call. The caller on the other side began speaking nervously about wanting to end her life. She did not want us to identify her. She had quit her job and dropped her classes. She was ready to drown herself into the unknown, which she thought would end her pain. We took the time to calm her down. We empathized with her as she spoke. She wouldn't disclose her reasons for wanting to die. She just wanted us to give her a reason to live. After about an hour on the phone, we managed to persuade her to identify herself. She agreed to a visit.

The next morning, a car pulled in our driveway. It was Sarah. As we invited her into our living room, she entered with a sunken face, visibly shaking hands, and no eye contact. She did not want to have anything to do with men, so she agreed to talk to me (Cynthia) alone. She narrated her ordeal and bitter experiences, and for four hours, I tried to calm her down, reassuring her of hope through Christ and my genuine love and concern for her. She decided to trust again. That was the beginning of her self-discovery and recovery.

As Sarah progressed in restoring her self-esteem, she went on to graduate successfully from pharmacy school and got married. We believe God planned for us to meet Sarah. Sometimes, we wonder what would have happened if our paths never crossed. Would Sarah have been alive? Maybe she would have found someone she could trust. But what if that didn't happen? Would she have still been battling with her depression? We ask ourselves, "How many Sarahs are out there waiting to cross paths with someone who will give them a thread to hang on?" Such nerve-wracking questions are a pointer to the realities of the battles and dire situations children of immigrant parents face. Sarah's parents almost lost a beautiful, talented daughter with a whole life ahead of her due to a cultural rift. The absence of a culturally tolerant environment almost resulted in a fatality. Her mom and dad's actions were not deliberate; they were being African.

Sarah's story birthed the writing of this book. It resulted in conductung research that involved a focus group of sixty young people, ranging between thirteen and twenty years, whose parents are African immigrants in the Columbus and Virginia districts of The Church of Pentecost, USA. We also interviewed twenty immigrant parents between the ages of forty-one and fifty-four to better understand their experiences and struggles as they raise their children in the West. The information we garnered from this study enabled us to recreate a multicultural and multigenerational story that spans several immigrant homes. It is a story of two diverging groups—the young and the old—children and their immigrant parents; multiple generations—Generation X and Millennial/Generation Z; and two cultures—African and Western, which have produced two worlds abiding under the same roof. These two diverging cultural worlds have created a platform for tension and misunderstanding in the African immigrant home. The conflict has also made it almost impossible for open and honest conversations between parents and their children. The war reveals the emotional struggles these children go through and how their African parents misunderstand their feelings and expression of them. On the other hand, it also shows African parents who feel disempowered and overrun by their children, thinking Western culture has had a negative influence on them.

Our several years of experience working as youth ministers, pastoring predominantly traditional African churches in North America, and raising three American-born kids have given us a firsthand experience of what it means to be African immigrant parents. On the other side of the spectrum, as we intimately became acquainted with the youth, we began to understand the cultural tension they must contend with. The exposure has strategically placed us at the crossroads of multiple cultures and generations, where we have gleaned much knowledge and experience on immigrant parent-child relationships.

In *Two-Worlds at War*, we take the reader into the world of the African immigrant family to explore the different facets of their world—two worlds defined by cultures and generations. Our goal is to help you identify the nature of these cultural differences to enhance your understanding of the tension these differences create. We also highlight the effects of these tensions and show immigrant families how to effectively bridge the cultural and generational gap using a blended cultural approach. Our message to parents emphasizes patience in parenting, tolerance, effective cross-cultural communication, and authentic love within the confines of biblical standards. We also point the youth to the reality of being at least two decades and a whole generation apart from their parents. This gap means that they and their parents live in two worlds under the same roof—worlds that are miles apart. The common space these two worlds share, however, suggests that though different, they are similar at heart. Hence, the diversity in both worlds should enrich families and improve relationships rather than result in a war. We hope that the information and experiences we share in this book would help promote healthy, loving relationships in African immigrant homes—homes that are not warring but winning.

If you find this book helpful, we hope you will share it with your African immigrant families and friends who may also be experiencing intergenerational and intercultural conflicts.

CHAPTER ONE

SAME HOME—TWO PERSPECTIVES

It is not our differences that divide us. It is our inability to recognize, accept, and celebrate those differences.—Audre Lorde

He sits in his room most of the time. He talks to his parents only when it is necessary. Ironically, he spends an endless amount of time gazing at his phone. He is lost in his world—a small world with invisible friends. But he also has a tiny visible world, consisting of a few friends from school and church. He connects with his world because that's where he finds acceptance, approval, and understanding. His parents do not understand the silence. They cannot comprehend the indifference he exhibits. Who is this *"he"*? His name is Sam, a sixteen-year-old African American-born young man with African immigrant parents. Sam lives with his parents and sibling in Arlington, Virginia.

Like many young people, Sam lives in a world outside of his parents' world. His parents migrated to the United States in the early nineties and had Sam and his sister, Erica. Life was normal when they were little kids, until Sam got to middle school and then high school. In his high school, he sees himself as different; others also see him as different. Sam becomes increasingly aware of the need to discover himself. He desires a comfortable niche that wouldn't consider him different and weird, with no racial disparities.

In another immigrant home in Worcester, Massachusetts, the rapid changes of adolescence are already taking hold of Barbara. Sixteen-year-old Barbara craves for more independence, and she is becoming more conscious of how others, especially her peers, see her. Typical of teenagers, she is trying desperately to fit in. The desire for acceptance from her peers makes her feel their opinions are much more important than her parents.' Therefore, Barbara is gradually developing her worldview—her culture. The new culture she embraces stands in stark contrast with the immigrant culture of her parents. She knows that. Her parents are starting to notice the changes in her tastes and preferences. They observe that she is beginning to place less emphasis on their culture. In response, her mom and dad feel threatened as they lose their parental authority. This situation is already creating tension in the home.

One Sunday morning, while the family is preparing for church, Barbara goes into her room. To get away from the loneliness at home, she starts connecting with her numerous online networks of friends. Her mother and father, on the other hand, feverishly get ready for church. To them, church attendance is mandatory if you live under their roof. When her mother sees no sign of Barbara coming out of her room, she goes in yelling as usual, *"Are you still here on that phone instead of getting ready for church?"*

Meanwhile, out of loneliness and desperation, Barbara has been posting alarming statements on her blog:

> *Why doesn't anyone understand me? I go out there and feel like the ugliest among my friends. Why am I so ugly? I look in the mirror, and I want to tear up my body. I do not have*

the perfect body. I am crushing within. My peers tell me I look weird, and I know that. I am not happy, and neither do my parents care about it. All they care about is going to work and making money. I am not worth anything, and everything they do proves that. No wonder they don't even have time for me and complain about everything I do, 'cos I am damned. At this point, all I care about is somebody to hold me, and for some reason, there's nobody. (crying)

Barbara's mother continues with her rambling without knowing the struggles her daughter is going through. She enters Barbara's room, seeing Barbara has the ripped blue jeans and a turquoise shirt she wore the day before on her bed. Her mom assumes that is what she is wearing to church. So yelling louder, she reminds Barbara of the inappropriate clothes she had on for a previous event, and she warns her: *"You dare not follow me with those ripped jeans to church today."* Barbara is sincerely frustrated with the escalating situation, but so is her mother. She doesn't have a choice, so eventually, she drags herself out of her bed and dresses up. She leaves home with pain and goes to church with her family.

As they arrive on the church premises, she waits for her parents to enter the sanctuary as she follows. Her eyes roam lazily through the auditorium, looking for a spot where she could find most of the youth and face the least judgmental looks. She finally finds her friend Abi. She sits next to her. At this point, Bible study is over, and they are entering into a time of praise. Abi begins engaging Barbara in a conversation:

"Hey, Barbara." Abi routinely hugs her. *"How are you?"*

Barbara does avoid eye contact with Abi. *"I'm okay."*

"You sure you are okay?" Abi questions. *"You don't look happy. What's going on?"*

"It's . . ." She begins but changes her mind. *"I am okay. It's just one of those things. I don't wanna talk about it now."*

Abi moves closer. *"Ohhh, it's sad to see you like this. Cheer up, and any time you wanna talk, know that I am around."*

"Okay, I will call you." Barbara agrees. *"Thanks, Abi. I appreciate it."*

Abi and Barbara join in the praise session. At this point, the praise and worship team is leading the congregation in mostly African songs. Most of the youth do not feel engaged because either they don't know the song, or they don't connect to it. They stand—disinterested. Throughout the service, Barbara fidgets on her phone, checking out messages on YouTube of her favorite online pastors. Though she is in a church room with over 300 members, she feels lonely. Barbara enters a sanctuary hoping to find peace, comfort, and answers to her troubled mind but leaves even more confused. Returning home, she reenters her world of darkness and confusion.

In Houston, Texas, Monica, a shy looking eighteen-year-old college freshman we spoke to, explained how she feels her parents do not understand her feelings. At college, parents of her room-mate, Meagan, visited often. Monica observed how her friend has an open and honest relationship with her parents and wondered why she couldn't have the same with hers. Besides, Monica was dealing with racial issues in her predominantly white college. The lack of support from home exacerbates her situation. She found safety and comfort in a Christian ministry off campus, where she fellowshipped frequently. That fellowship was more youth oriented and relevant to her generation. When she returned home on vacation, she found everything wrong with her church because it looked different from what she experienced on campus. Now she does not feel enthusiastic about attending church or engaging her parents. She finds herself arguing a lot more with them. All of this is causing tension at home.

We see slightly different shades of these cultural tensions in several immigrant households. These are homes where parents often train their children with African cultural norms and values. In her book, *"Raising an African Child in America: From the Perspective of an Immigrant Nigerian Mom"* Marcellina Oparaoji mentions these values as including hard work, resilience, respect for authority, caring for self and siblings, assuming assigned roles in the home, love of family, and patriotism.[1] Contrarily, these children grow up in another culture, the Western culture that focuses on education, confidence, self-assertion, fearlessness, and outspokenness.[2] In these homes, children are in one world, and parents are in another—and these worlds are miles apart!

> *The generation one belongs to defines the person's ethical, moral, social, and religious stances, and these carry profound impacts on family structures, faith, and values.*

We Are Different

Generations come and go. Each generation carries its unique norms, preferences, and trends. The generation one belongs to defines the person's ethical, moral, social, and religious stances, and these carry profound impacts on family structures, faith, and values. Five major generations exist, which include the traditionalists, the Baby Boomers, Generation X, Millennials, and Generation Z.[3,4]

In the United States, the Baby Boomers had strict parents, who were the traditionalists. They passed on their toughness to their Boomer children. When Boomers became parents, they used the toughness they learned from their parents to create dual-career homes, raising their children in two-career families or single-parent households. Boomer parents worked long hours and had less time for their kids—Generation X.[5]

Growing up, Generation Xers experienced lots of struggles, moral authority, and an attitude of the "parent is right." They objected to their parents' overly strict parenting and determined to create a more liberal parental style and legacy for their children, who are the Millennials and Generation Z.[6] Millennials and subsequent generations have had extensive parental involvement, which has resulted in a mentality of immediacy. It is no wonder that people see Millennials as the "laziest generation." They build their truth and are not bound by the traditions and dictates of their parents, unlike previous generations.[7] Shaw describes them:

> They won't get off their phones. They aren't loyal. They don't show respect. They are naïve about what it takes to make organizations work. They are impatient and drop out if you don't implement their ideas. They are materialistic and think they are entitled. They've grown up in a sex-saturated world. They are walking away from Christianity. They want meaning and they want authenticity.[8]

The stark differences between the generational groups suggest that for the contemporary Western family, parents and their children are likely to differ on several grounds. For the immigrant family, the disparity is more complicated, because, besides the generational differences, they must deal with cultural differences. For such families, these dynamics often put parents in one world, and their children in another world. Besides the generational and cultural differences, factors such as secularism, postmodernism, and technology further widen the gap between parents and their children. The diverging worlds mean diverging values and ways of life.

A New World

Over 20 years ago, two Stanford PhD students created Google, Tamagotchi toys were a worldwide phenomenon, and *Harry Potter and the Sorcerer's Stone* hit shelves for the first time. A decade later, in 2007, Netflix launched its video streaming service, Instagram didn't exist, and most of us were still using flip phones.[9]

The average Western parent admits that the world has changed in many ways. From a world with flip phones in the 1990s, we now see a fast-paced, techno world where companies release new phones multiple times a year. Our society has transitioned from videotape to streaming to digital streaming on the go, and a no-internet world, to one with broadband home internet access. It is a new world, a trendy one.

For the immigrant family still trying to fit into the Western culture, the world is even newer. It is a world where values that were important to parents seem to lose their significance. It is a world where children are sexualized earlier than previous generations were. Thirteen-year-olds are already asking questions that, in the past, only adults would ask. Nine-year-old children are already talking about their sexualities and discussing having crushes. It's a world in which children know more than presumed. Contrarily, most immigrant parents can't come to terms with the extent of exposure that their children have. Hence, instead of engaging their children, they somehow pretend as if they are oblivious to the tides and currents of the new world and its effects on their children:

> *They don't listen, and when they do, it's only to tell me I am wrong. They don't get that we are in a different world.*

> —*Ama, seventeen years old.*

> *My parents overreact when I confess something to them. They fail to understand my life as a teenage girl growing up in America, and they make wrong judgments about me, so, it's hard to go to them when I have issues.*

> —*Belinda, sixteen years old.*

These sentiments were shared among the youth who feel their immigrant parents don't take the time to listen to them as they find their place in a world that is different from what they know from home. Ours is a world with anti-Christian views. Such views are gradually becoming the norm of society, making it difficult for the Christian immigrant family who desires to raise their children according to biblical standards and their cultural values. It is a world of computers and games, a world of immediacy and relative truth, and one that is different from what most traditional parents know. It is a world that questions everything.

At the age of five, our son was asking some intriguing questions. At this tender age, he wanted to understand the reason for the things we ask him to do. In 2003, I (George) was a middle school teacher, teaching Algebra in Greensboro, North Carolina. I had just moved to the States, and it was my first teaching appointment. I did not understand the cultural dynamics at the time, having been in the country for barely a year. With my Ghanaian cultural background, I expected the middle schoolers to respond to me and behave like those I taught at the junior high school (middle school) in Ghana. I had a cultural shock when one young girl asked me, *"Why?"* for every single instruction I gave the class. I was frustrated, but she seemed not to be bothered. After all, that was the norm in middle school classrooms. I quickly had to learn that it was reasonable for a student to question a teacher, and more importantly, the teacher was required to explain. I learned at the speed of light that in America, children's rights are equivalent to adults' rights. It was a different world! Thankfully, I did not have any children of my own then because it would've been a disaster if they questioned my authority.

Similarly, in the average immigrant family, a subtle war begins in the hearts of both parents and their youthful children. Parents are frustrated that their children are losing interest in church. They are disturbed that their children are acting in ways that are concerning. As parents, they feel helpless because they don't understand their children and feel disrespected by them. They attempt to bridge the cultural gap using strategies they know; however, these fall short, or worse, backfire. The result is often tension in the home leading to broken parent-child relationships.

We suggest that to combat this war within the walls of immigrant families, both parents and children should acknowledge their differences and believe that they can work through them.

In the face of the seeming hopelessness, we strive to present a ray of hope to such parents that all is not lost. For these parents, our message is that all things are possible if they believe (Mark 9:23). We suggest that to combat this war within the walls of immigrant families, both parents and children should acknowledge their differences and believe that they can work through them. Immigrant parents need the knowledge and necessary awareness to better adjust to the Western environment, which will enable them to meet their children in a middle way, rather than expecting their children to act like them. This mindset also requires that parents acknowledge that they live in a new world, and the only way to adjust to the newness is for them to be open to the reality of the new life, a life of individualism, self-assertion, and freedom. Parents must realize that they must engage with their young ones, who are assimilating into the culture of this new world at a faster rate. In the "new world," children must also be willing to understand and cooperate with their parents. As both parties agree to work together, they will collaboratively learn and unlearn certain aspects of their respective cultures, which will enable them to converge somewhere in between.

A Cry for Autonomy

Jojo is only seventeen. His parents are facing a common dilemma. Until Jojo went to high school, he depended on his parents for most of the decisions about his life. He communicated with them regularly and engaged them in his daily life. But for whatever reason, seventeen-year-old Jojo has changed. Jojo returns home from school and goes straight to his room and shuts the door. His parents, Uncle Mark and Auntie Lizzy, complain bitterly, saying, "It's like he wants to shut us out of his life."

Most parents are struggling with these kinds of abrupt changes in attitudes from their children. For immigrant parents who grew in communal cultures, such reactions can be shocking! Parents may find themselves at a crossroads. Suddenly, they realize that their daughter has withdrawn from everyone in the family, and she prefers to spend her leisure hours just on social media with unknown friends. Without understanding her, they may think she has something terrible to hide, but this may not necessarily be so. Instead, she probably wants a life of her own—some privacy, as dictated by the culture. At this stage, young people may be less likely to participate in family and social events, which may be surprising to parents. Still, yes, it's a new world, and the rules of the 1980s have lost some relevance.

In this new world, the definition of freedom is different from what parents knew it to be. What parents may be seeing in their children is a quest for autonomy and identity in a new culture. As the youth transition into adulthood, they explore their developmental processes and learn to be assertive. Some parents may not understand these changes and brand a youth who is going through these transitions as disrespectful or arrogant. But it might be that they are just growing up. It is a stage where most young people do not even understand their emotions or reactions. For such young people, growing in a home with multiple cultures further complicates matters.

An Added Layer of Conflict

We cannot ignore the intergenerational tension that exists in Western homes; however, for immigrant families coming from Africa, Asia, or another culture, the conflict can be more intense and more dividing. Such immigrants suddenly find themselves in a completely different environment in a quest for greener pastures. As immigrant families lose their support systems and take on multiple jobs, their living conditions become increasingly difficult. They have bills to pay in addition to the added responsibility of sending money to relatives in their respective home countries.

Meanwhile, the children whom they migrate with gradually shed the communal and authoritative lifestyle. They embrace a culture that is individualistic and permissive. These children enter the school system and adjust to the mainstream culture at a much faster rate than their parents. Children who are born into the mainstream culture submerge themselves in the culture even faster. Their food preferences, language, clothing, and religious views begin to take on a different form.

These complex cultural dynamics mean that immigrant families face two opposing worlds—worlds divided by generations and cultures. They must not only adjust to the intergenerational differences in a new environment, but also learn to negotiate between two cultural worlds: Western culture and African culture. As a result of these difficulties, immigrant families struggle to coexist peacefully. These challenges have adverse effects on the harmony of family units and the destiny of children of immigrant parents.

> *These complex cultural dynamics mean that immigrant families face two opposing worlds—worlds divided by generations and cultures.*

Amid the multiple layers of complexities in immigrant homes, how can such families in the West find common grounds of understanding and coexistence? This question raises further questions: In immigrant households in the West, how can families contain different generational and cultural worldviews? How do they manage them so that tension and conflict do not ruin treasured parent-child relationships?

In this book, we take the immigrant parent into the "obscure" world of their youthful children and usher the youth into the "weird" world of their parents, respectively. We consider why these *two worlds are at war* and then explore common grounds for coexistence.

CHAPTER TWO

WE ARE NOT JUST DECADES APART

I suppose every generation has a conceit of itself which elevates it, in its own opinion, above that which comes after it.—Margaret Wilson Oliphant

"Michael, where do you think you are going in those clothes?" Michael's mom, Abigail, questions. *"Why can't you listen to what I have to say?"*

[Michael is silent]

"Am I talking to a tree? Abigail adds. "Won't you respond?"

"But Mom . . ."

"Shut up." Abigail silences Michael.

"Mom, that was why I was quiet. I knew if I opened my mouth, you would shut me up. These clothes are okay. It's the trend."

"What trend?" At this point, Abigail is getting furious. *"Is that how a Christian should dress?"*

"Mom, everyone at my school wears it. Some of my friends at church have these types of clothes as well. Why don't you get it? There is nothing wrong with these."

"I am mad; that is why I don't get it. I am crazy." Abigail is quickly losing her temper. *"I have been your age before. I have lived the life you are living, and I know all the consequences of your lifestyle. When I was your age, I dared not even think of having these clothes in my closet."*

"But Mom, there is nothing wrong with them. Why do you always judge me?"

"There is everything wrong with these, Michael. See how your thighs are showing in those holes in the trousers. And your top is too unkempt. You look like a mad person if you care to know. Come on, go back to your room and change."

"There is nothing wrong with this shirt and pants, Mom."

"Your friend Kwame doesn't dress like that. You see how he dresses so nicely all the time. He is such a gentleman."

"There you go again, Mom; I hate these comparisons. Why can't you stop it? You have no idea what he does in secret. You think he is a good boy, huh?"

[Michael fumes]

"You think he is better than me, huh." Michael questions. *"I am sorry, but I don't think you are gonna like any of my clothes. As for those you got for me the other day, I put them in the box you are shipping back to Ghana because they are too big on me."*

"You did what, Michael? Nonsense. So, you think you know better than me or what? Don't you know I came to America first, and that is why you are here? I will show you that I am your mom. This whole American culture is driving you all crazy. I am so frustrated with you."

"Enough of this crap. I am sick and tired of being reminded about all this." Michael begins to walk away.

"Ahhh! You call me trash? I would have given you a dirty slap if you were standing next to me."

"I did not call you trash. I just meant I don't like your judging me and making me feel as if I don't have a say in this house." Michael keeps walking away from his mother, not wanting to say another word.

"This American craziness has gotten into your head, and you think you are the boss of this house. I will show you that you are in America because of me."

[Michael rushes to his room in anger]

What could make an immigrant parent disapprove of a dress code, food choice, or hairstyle, which may be completely fine for a younger generation child from the mainstream Western culture? And how do children of immigrant parents reconcile the

seemingly harsh and overly strict attitudes of their parents, com-
pared to the more laid-back parenting styles of the family across
the block?

Michael is a nineteen-year-old junior who just returned from
college. Born in Ghana, Michael arrived in the United States with
his parents when he was only six. He has grown in America and
adopted its way of life, values, and mannerisms. His parents relo-
cated to America from Ghana thirteen years ago. Michael's mom,
Abigail, is a forty-two-year-old who has managed to go through the
college system in the United States to become a nurse. Nonetheless,
she has maintained much of her Ghanaian culture and beliefs.
Likewise, Michael's dad, a radiologist, has a similar cultural stance.
They both believe that American culture is too liberal. Hence, they
try to teach or impose the Ghanaian culture on their son Michael
and his siblings. Abigail, Michael's mom, expresses her sentiments
in the interview:

> *We have our culture, and we came to meet the American cul-
> ture. What I know all my life, and what my parents trained
> me with, is the Ghanaian culture. It has made me a good
> woman, and I want to teach my children the same culture
> so that they will turn out good. But here in America, you
> can't beat your child. Sometimes, if you yell, they say you are
> abusing your child. Our children are now so American that
> they feel shy speaking our language, and they don't want to
> eat our food sometimes. What annoys me is the way they dress.
> And if you talk about it, they think you don't understand.*

Michael's mom also expresses similar sentiments that her friend,
thirty-eight-year-old Faustina, shared with her. Faustina has three
children. The oldest, who is thirteen, is an eighth grader. She
expressed the concern that despite how much she tries, her daughter
can't get along with her. She wishes she could communicate

better and more often with her without arguing, but that never seems possible.

In another immigrant home, Yaw, who is sixteen, experiences the same cultural dynamics. He believes the gap between him and his parents is because his parents are stuck in their premigration cultures. They are resistant to change. In our youth focus group discussion on immigrant parents and their children, we posed a question on the extent to which they feel their parents understand them. Yaw had this to say:

> *My parents assume we are all terrible kids and feel they need to keep fixing us up. They don't give us the benefit of the doubt. They judge us by the way we dress and all that, but that's just fashion. That's not who we are. All they know is African culture. They don't even care to see that we were born here, so we can't be like them.*

Claudia, another girl in the discussion, added:

> *It's so hard to grow up as an immigrant kid. Knowing where you fit in remains a battle all your life. They don't get that we can't behave the way they did when they were growing up. They forget that times have changed.*

Immigrants who relocate to a new country must embrace two cultures—their native culture and the host culture. While some first-generation immigrants[10] migrate with their children from their native countries, others give birth in the host nation. Whether these children are born into the host culture or not, they are more likely to adopt the host culture and language much faster than their parents.[11] Immigrant parents, on the other hand, often struggle to adapt to the new culture.[12]

Parents often migrate with the hope to gain a better lifestyle for their families. In response, they expect a cordial and reciprocal relationship with their children in the new environment as it existed in their home country. Hardly do they anticipate the extreme cultural shock and the difficulty in adjusting to an entirely new culture. This cultural shock is due to the more permissive way of life that allows for increased self-assertiveness versus the more strict and controlled culture they know. As a parent, if you are not fluent in the English language, this adds another layer of complication. Further, it limits communication with your child(ren) and your ability to navigate the complex school, economic, and social systems.

The differences that ensue between immigrant parents and their children because of the multiple cultures they must deal with in a new environment is like

> *The differences that ensue between immigrant parents and their children because of multiple cultures they must deal with in a new environment is like mixing multiple cultures, age groups, and generations in the same bowl.*

mixing multiple cultures, age groups, and generations in the same bowl. Rather than getting a perfectly mixed and smooth substance, the result is a substance with each item floating separately, just like when you combine water and oil. The contents do not mix because the ingredients in it are so different—in terms of generations, languages, preferences, and expectations.

Decades Apart

Each generation is distinctively different from the subsequent one. Each thinks the generation preceding it "doesn't get it." Why doesn't each generation understand the other at any point in life? The bottom line is that the average age gap between two generations is about twenty to thirty years. So many changes can occur in twenty or thirty years! Due to these changes, parents and their children may have similar beliefs and values. Still, their meaning and expression—which are contextual and influenced by events of that generation—may differ. For instance, even if parents and their children are educated, the way parents learned may be different from how their children are learning. Parents read from books, and their children are reading from tablets. Parents memorized. Their children are getting their information from Google. Parents typed words. Their children are typing emojis. The generational gap causes a lot of misunderstanding and conflicts at home, with adverse effects on parent-child relationships.

From our study, we observed that what complicates these generational dynamics even more for the African immigrant family is that the parents we focused on—who mostly fall into the category of Generation X—have a mindset like the Baby Boomer generation in the host culture. Both generations are similar in terms of their limited access to information, work schedules, and inability to spend enough time with their kids. Besides, both groups are somewhat protective and pushy. Nonetheless, whereas Baby Boomers range between fifty-six and seventy-five years, Generation X, which we focus on is between forty-one and fifty-four years old.

Immigrant parents are, therefore, raising their Millennial and Generation Z kids with parenting styles and ideals of Boomers who sit about two decades apart from them. This development is happening in a cultural environment that is not entirely familiar to them. That is to say that such parents have a Baby Boomer mindset—which is an entire generation behind! And what compli-cates things is that they are raising children who are surrounded by friends and acquaintances that are raised by Generation X parents with a Generation X mindset. The gap between the values and ideals of immigrant parents and the expectations of their children presents two conflicting and almost disagreeable worlds, with par-ents on one side and children on the other side—worlds with dif-ferent views, different lifestyles, and in essence, different cultures.

The Cultural Divide

Most immigrants maintain their culture, language, and values in their new environments. In some instances, some immigrants may hold onto their premigration values. However, the same may have changed since they left their home country. Such people believe these values are magnets that hold the family unit together. So they see the new culture as threatening this cohesiveness and presenting ideas that contradict their strongly upheld values and the unity of the family.

The values of the African immigrant culture are different from the permissive Western culture in many ways. As an African immi-grant parent, you have children who may have been born or raised in Western culture. However, as you slowly learn the new culture, your children, quickly submerge themselves in it, almost entirely. The cultural clash results in generational conflict, which occurs when children adopt the Western way of life, and at the same time, lose their parents' native culture. The cultural divide causes a lot of tension in many African immigrant homes, with several psycholog-ical and spiritual effects. The nature of the tension, however, depends on how well parents and children adjust in the new culture. The more immigrant parents hold on to their native cultures and values, the more they may struggle with the cultural differences in their new surroundings.

The children of immigrant parents must grapple with growing up in one culture yet expected to behave in the way of another culture. Immigrants from other countries such as China, Mexico, India, and Vietnam have managed to maintain their indigenous cultures while permeating through Western cultural systems. They have carved successful niches, which have helped to safeguard their cultures and language. Hence, for such people, life in the host country is an extension of life in the homeland, though they may still have some struggles. For the African immigrant in the diaspora, however, the lack of a community-oriented way of submerging children in their native culture presents a difficult challenge in their efforts to combine both cultures.

The children of immigrant parents must grapple with growing up in one culture yet expected to behave in the way of another culture.

In the African immigrant home, cultural differences play out in the usual ways of living, such as dressing, relationships, friendships, communication, and spiritual life. Immigrant parents keep a keen eye on the choice of friends and acquaintances and issues such as dating and outings. Such surveillance may outrage their children. The cultural dynamics may also lead to a lot of misunderstandings in communication. For instance, a youth who is confident might be considered proud and rebellious. On the other hand, a Millennial or Generation Z teenage girl might question specific actions from her parents. But these kinds of questioning often result in less desirable outcomes.

Abigail, a nineteen-year old, is upstairs when her mom calls her. She responds but stays upstairs for another ten minutes before coming down because she wanted to finish up with what she was doing. However, before Abigail could step onto the wooden stairs and walk down to the kitchen where she thought her mother was, her mom yells even louder:

"Abi, didn't you hear me calling you?"

"Yes, Mommy. Abigail responds. *"I am coming."*

"How many times would I call before you respond?" Abigail's mother queries.

[Abi gets downstairs and realizes that her mommy was sitting in the living room, talking to a friend on the phone.]

"Abi, get me a bottle of water from the kitchen."

[Abi shakes her head secretly, wondering why her mother will call her from upstairs to get the water when where she is sitting is closer to where the water is. She gets the water, nonetheless, and gives it to her.]

"Mom, here you go."

"Why have you made that face?" Abigail's mom asks.

"Nothing."

"What do you mean by nothing? So you will act up like that when you have to get me water? What is wrong with you?"

"Mommy, it's nothing, I was just wondering why I had to come down to get the water which is close to you."

"Nonsense. Are you to tell me what to do? So, you have a problem with getting water for your mother to drink. You are lucky. When I was in Ghana, I used to carry water for miles for the family. You are getting water in the same house, and you are complaining. Don't get on my nerves."

[Abigail walks away silently]

Similarly, in our focus group session, Amanda explained how often her mom speaks to her harshly when she wants her to wash the dishes:

Amanda, you must wash those dishes before we head to church. And don't tell me you will do it later. You have to do it now.

—Eighteen years old

After washing the dishes, Amanda walks into her room and slams the door behind her, in defiance. She feels her mom does not understand her and doesn't know how she feels when she yells at her like that. Amanda had decided not to go to church that day because of her mom's authoritarian parenting approach. She feels if no one else would understand her struggles, her mom should. But she doesn't. Instead, she thinks her rules will straighten Amanda up and prevent her from falling prey to the bad habits of Western culture. But the same rules are pushing Amanda away. In Amanda's home, the leading causes of such conflicts and misunderstandings stem from how values and cultures have evolved; hence, what mom deems unacceptable may be completely fine in Amanda's culture. So, Amanda and her parents share the same space, but they are worlds apart! Similarly, Michael expresses his frustration about the seemingly bossy nature of his dad in another instance from the focus group:

Last summer, I couldn't believe what my dad did! I woke up one day to find out that he had cut my hair. I was wearing an afro with cropped sides, and he had asked me to go to the barber and have it redone since he felt it was a ghetto haircut. After he cut my hair, I felt so depressed and shy to go out, so I stayed indoors for a couple of days until my hair began to grow. I hated my dad for doing that to me, but I dared not complain.

In this instance, waking up to realize his hair has been cut threw Michael into a state of depression or a feeling of low self-esteem. This act could also lead to animosity between him and his dad. Simple dialogue and mutual understanding, however, could have achieved the intended results and prevented any potential adverse consequences.

Such generational misunderstanding and tension within immigrant communities are common, and they go beyond the home to even the church environment. One of our pastor friends once shared how a young seventeen-year-old lady came up to give a testimony at a church gathering where the congregation was a mostly older, traditional generation. As the young lady went on, she began making references to the leaders and congregation as *"you guys"* and *"thank you, guys,"* to the surprise of some of the congregants. The pastor, on the other hand, did not see the use of that language as disrespectful because he understood the Western culture. Another parent who is either adamant or not too familiar with the terms may rebuke such a person.

Several African parents do not want to hear the word *"hey,"* which means "hello" in Western culture, because to them, the phrase suggests yelling. Tony narrated his experience on a sunny Saturday afternoon with his father:

"Hey, Daddy, when are we going out to get the stuff from Home Depot? We need to fix the lawn lights," Tony asks his father.

"How many times should I tell you not to use this 'hey' 'hey' thing on me? Tony's father reacted furiously. *"Don't you know it is disrespectful to use 'hey' on an adult? Why would you yell at me like that?"*

"Daddy, it's not like that. Tony tries to explain himself. *"I am sorry, I was just calling out for you."*

"I have told you repeatedly. If you don't stop, you will take it out, and people will think you don't respect."

"But daddy, that is unreasonable. 'Hey' isn't bad, and I don't see why somebody would brand me as disrespectful just for using 'hey.'" Tony further attempts to convince his father.

"There you go again. You have an answer for everything I say. You think you know everything, and you are calling me unreasonable. You are telling me I am not making sense. When will you learn to respect?"

[Tony is silent.]

Tony kept quiet because he didn't want his responses to upset his dad. He apologized and went upstairs to his room. While there, he lazily lay on his messy bed and gazed into the ceiling. As he lay there with his knees bent, eyes towards the ceiling, and hands behind his head, his mind wondered about the two diverging worlds existing under his roof. He reflected on stories shared by his non-African friends at school, which are entirely different from his own experiences. Jason, his Caucasian friend, has casual conversations with his father all the time and plays basketball with him. Alex, his African American friend (both of Alex's parents were born in the United States), can easily say no to his mommy, and she would understand without a flinch. In Tony's home, however, such behavior is unacceptable. As he forces himself to take a nap, he slips into dreamland, only to awake to the realities of the two worlds in his home.

Like Tony, when youth feel they cannot connect to their immigrant parents' culture, so many thoughts run through their minds. They view their parents as proponents of a culture that takes away their freedom. In such situations, resentment begins to build up within them, which negatively affects the family unit. The point we are making here is not to say the African culture is flawed, and so the youth should entirely adopt Western culture. Instead, we suggest the need for parents to understand that the behaviors these children exhibit are due to their sheer presence in another culture—they do not have control over this choice. As a parent, having that mindset will help you to know that some of the slang your children use, or the way they act may not be necessarily wrong. You will begin to understand that your children are just different from what you know. Such knowledge will also help you to patiently work with them to identify elements of the more culturally appealing aspects of Western culture and blend that with the African culture.

Instead, we suggest the need for parents to understand that the behaviors these children exhibit are due to their sheer presence in another culture—they do not have control over this choice.

Our Two Worlds

Abena is a Ghanaian American. Born in Ghana, her parents brought her to the United States when she was only three. Now eighteen, she identifies more with the mainstream American culture than her African roots. Likewise, seventeen-year old American-born Tony, who attends a predominantly white high school, has been influenced so much by the youthful mainstream culture. His dad can't have this, and there is a constant tension between them. The cultural differences between Abena and her parents and Tony and his father highlighted here are enough to produce specific responses that can potentially widen the relationship gap between parents and children in immigrant homes.

Parenting involves providing for the physical, emotional, social, and intellectual development of a child from infancy to adulthood. It is a daily journey that impacts a child's identity. Parenting style may be the most critical factor in determining the behavioral patterns, character, decision making, and ultimate destiny of young people. Prov. 22:6 admonishes parents to train up their children in the way they should go, and when they are old, they will not depart from it. Parents are, therefore, to provide the necessary nurturing and mentoring to ensure the successful development of their children.

In the Western environment, the average child spends more time outside the home, either at school or with friends. Even when they are home, they spend more time on social media, TV, or movies. They are exposed more to external forces than their parents were. A news report found that teens spend a lot of time watching TV, gaming, reading, listening to music, and on social media. Specifically, on any given day, teens in the United States spend about nine hours using media. That is more time than the time they typically spend sleeping and more time than they spend with their parents and teachers. The youth of today are therefore surrounded by a network of visible and invisible friends and influencers, who are mostly digitally based and often physically unknown.

According to Kelly Wallace, a news reporter on CNN, "Kids live in this massive 24/7 digital media technology world, and it's shaping every aspect of their life." In a Westernized and postmodern environment, most of the tenets of this massive influence contradict the traditional African values. The children of African immigrants quickly develop a Western-style value system. These values counter the essential ideals of African immigrants' conservative Christian values.

The traditional African values are top-down in the way parents communicate to their children. There are, however, exceptions, for homes where parents may be exposed to a global parenting trend.

The two worlds battle over several issues—the worlds represent a clash of two major cultural perspectives with opposing languages, values, and beliefs.

In most African home, parents hardly consider the child's opinion in decision making. Besides, the adult may become uncomfortable or feel insulted when a child expresses his or her opinion. Your father determines who can be your friend and who cannot. He tells you the academic courses you can choose to do in school. Your mother carefully examines your outfit before you leave the house. The time you sleep and wake are all monitored. The fear of punishment keeps the child submissive for the most part. That is the parenting style that some immigrant parents went through growing up in their respective countries of origin.

The challenge, though, is that as an African parent, your child did not go through this African training and cultural upbringing with you. In the West, the marks of tolerance, permissiveness, individuality, and independence are an integral component of our contemporary culture that have become shared values among the youthful generation. The Western culture preaches freedom and personal space, and the youth strive to find their own identity. Hence, whereas the Christian beliefs of immigrant parents call for strict adherence to biblical values and standards, their children believe something else: tolerance and permissiveness. Therefore, they struggle to pattern their lives exactly after the cultural values of their parents.

These divergent views create an environment of misunderstanding, confusion, and tension. It's an environment in which parents believe they are right. The child feels they are also correct, and their parents just don't get it. The two worlds battle over several issues—the worlds represent a clash of two major cultural perspectives with opposing languages, values, and beliefs.

Language

Language is an essential element in the immigrant culture. Language serves as a means of communication and a carrier of culture.[13] Immigrant parents, who usually prefer to speak their native languages, too often prefer that their first-generation American-born children adopt the African language over the English language. However, these children have grown up in the West. Hence, much of what they know is the dominant culture, with its English language. Their parents often feel they could abandon their African language by embracing too much of the Western culture and its language.

Some African parents may insist that their children speak their native language at home and the English language at school. However, for the immigrant kid, the transition between speaking the native language at home and English at school can be difficult. Also, some children may regard the language spoken at home as inferior, simply because many of their mainstream peers are unfamiliar with it.

Most young people feel uncomfortable when their parents speak the English language with an ethnic accent, especially in public. Mary, a twenty-one-year old senior we encountered, narrated her experience when she had come home on vacation. She went to hang out with three of her friends, Maegan, Sarah, and Kelly, who are Caucasians, and African American, respectively. The girls came to drop her home. When they arrived, Mary's mom was stepping out of the house. She immediately started speaking Twi, a Ghanaian language, to her daughter Mary, who was getting out of the car. Mary narrated her embarrassment because her friends began quizzing, *"What kind of language is that?"* She pretended not to have heard her mom and rushed inside the house.

McKenzie, a fourteen-year-old middle schooler similarly expressed her ordeal about a day her mom visited her school during the focus group discussion:

> *Oh, my goodness, I was so embarrassed. My mom came to school one day for a parent-teacher conference. Just when she finished and we were walking down the school hallway, she got a phone call, and at that point, I knew I was dead. She was yelling on the phone as usual, and everyone was looking at us. I was like, "Wait! What? Seriously?"*

She went ahead to narrate that when they got out of the building and her mother was done with the talking on the phone, she spoke to her:

> *"Mommy, that was a bit too loud. Everyone was looking at us."*

"What do you mean?" her mom quizzed. *"I was talking on the phone; don't they also talk on the phone? What is wrong with that?"*

"I know you can talk on the phone, but your voice was too loud; everyone was just staring, and I felt bad," McKenzie responds, looking on her phone.

"Ahhhh! Did you feel bad? What does that mean? You feel shy about being Ghanaian? Instead of being ashamed that I was yelling, you should be ashamed of being ashamed of your heritage. Don't even repeat that stupid thing to me again." McKenzie's mother angrily walks away towards the parking lot.

"I didn't mean to upset you. McKenzie follows her mother from a distance. *"It's just that it feels weird."*

"Just shut up, because you are making me mad," McKenzie's mother yells at her as she enters the car. *"Whether you like it or not, you are Ghanaian. You are not a White person; you are a Ghanaian. I will speak Twi with you anytime I come here, and try and complain again, you will see what will happen to you."*

McKenzie sits in the back seat of the car and fidgets on her phone. She couldn't wait to get home.

McKenzie said that after that long lecture, she wished she had kept quiet. The following day, she had to feign sickness to skip school because she wasn't ready for the interrogation from her friends and the looks from everyone that saw them.

Culture is essential in every context, and one major component of culture is language. The push from immigrant parents for their children to learn their language is good because, after all, your ability to speak a second language gives you an added advantage. However, young people don't appreciate it if parents mandate them to speak the second language in front of other people who may not be familiar with the language, especially their peers, who could make fun of them. This doesn't mean they dislike the ethnic language. Our survey indicated that most African youth identified themselves, first, with their parents' home country and then being Americans. Similarly, at an international day event at our church, we observed this cultural preference. While we called out several countries such as Guinea, Guyana, Haiti, Nigeria, and Sierra Leone, all the youth, including those born in America, identified first with their parents' countries. Interestingly, when we called out America, all of them responded as well. So, the reality is that the youth associate with African culture and the language. But they don't want to look different before their peers.

Differences in how immigrant parents and their children understand mainstream language can also arouse tension and misunderstanding. For example, in most African homes, you dare not tell an adult, "Don't be silly. This phrase may sound rude. However, the same expression means "Don't be funny" in Western culture. Similarly, an immigrant parent may misunderstand "bruh," which is common in everyday language in the mainstream culture. So, whereas, such expressions are ordinary outside of the home, they are considered taboo as the child enters the home domain The different interpretations of language further create misunderstanding and tension in immigrant households.

Sharing a linguistic code is very necessary for the effective exercise of parental authority. So, an issue related to language in immigrant homes is how the difference in language proficiency between parents and children affects parental control at home. In homes where there is a communication gap between parents and their children, because children can't speak their parents' native language and vice versa, parents are limited in how they can adequately support their children. Where parents are not fluent in English, some children often play the role of translators and cultural mediators for their families. This situation shifts their positions, and parents lose a certain level of authority. The role-play can potentially disturb the "normal balance" of parent-child relationships. Youth who play these adult roles may be hesitant to rely on their parents for some help. These occurrences contradict the native culture, which presents the parent as having the final say and knowing it all, which adds another layer of complexity to the immigrant parent-child relationship.

Parental Respect or Mutual Respect

A new cultural environment comes with changes in expectations and relationship dynamics between immigrant parents and their children. The perspective of immigrant parents on the meaning of respect and honor may be starkly different from that of their children. In African culture, the adult is always right. As ultimate decision-makers, they expect children to conform to parental demands without dispute. Gloria expresses her frustration on this cultural position:

> *Because I am the oldest, I do all the chores and most of the work in the house that an adult will do, but I can't talk back.*

> *—Gloria, nineteen years old*

Gloria is considered old enough to do a lot of the chores at home but not old enough to express herself. Such perspectives contradict the experiences and beliefs of the youth on what they have learned in Western culture as constituting respect. Immigrant parents believe that adapting to the new culture often results in a loss of traditional African values. They, therefore, try to instill these values into their Western-bred children. Ironically, these children firmly uphold child rights, reasoning, and questioning. The differences in views result in a clash of value systems. To the youth, what their parents consider to be disrespectful is just fine in the mainstream culture.

It's quite interesting that while most immigrant parents are less willing to embrace Western cultural beliefs on parental authority, a lot of children appreciate the African culture's emphasis on respect and honor for the elderly. The question is that if the youth like their parents' immigrant culture, why are they not receptive to specific values and practices associated with their parents' way of life? The

The question is that if the youth like their parents' immigrant culture, why are they not receptive to specific values and practices associated with their parents' way of life?

Bible admonishes children to respect older people: "You shall stand up before the gray head and honor the face of an old man" (Lev. 19:32) and to honor their father and mother (Eph. 6:1). But how far should children take this honor? Does honoring mean that you have no say at all? Does it mean you must take everything from your parents, regardless of how you feel about it? Does it mean the absence of questioning?

As young parents, we were hit by the reality of the divergent views on parental respect when our first child turned two and could talk. Instead of the expected *"Yes, Mommy"* or *"Yes, Daddy,"* she would often ask *"Why?"* That was not what we expected, even though we had experienced firsthand the questioning aspect of Western culture. We often rebuked her for what we considered to be disrespectful at an early age. The more we acquainted ourselves with the American culture and engaged in the youth ministry, the more we became increasingly aware of the divergence between our expectations and the realities of Western culture. The exposure allowed us to reorient our mentality and align our expectations to the cultural realities on the ground. This position is not the same stance as compromising scripturally accepted standards. We decided to make this adjustment from a biblical stance, while still upholding our cherished African cultural values of respect and honor.

Often, our culture dictates our actions. The meaning of respect and honor is different for the African parent and their children. The way each generation understands these values determine how they act them out. As an immigrant parent, it might, therefore, be unrealistic to expect your child to behave and respond completely like an African because they are growing in a Western cultural context. This expectation breeds a lot of confusion, which leads to parent-child conflicts. Several youth have suffered psychological and social disorders due to these conflicts, which we discuss in Chapter 5. One significant way to minimize such effects with the associated emotional stresses is to find common grounds of understanding, based on love and honest communication.

Love and Affection

Anabel, a forty-two-year-old immigrant mother we once spoke to, explained how she reacted to affection toward her son. When her first son was five, he would often kiss his mom goodnight. Since Anabel was not used to giving and receiving love, she responded in a way that made her son uncomfortable. As her son grew up, he recognized his mom's discomfort and stopped the demonstration of love. Anabel recounts with deep regrets that she realized how different her son, who is now eighteen, is from his younger brother and sister. She learned her lesson. She decided to give affection to her two younger children, which improved their self-confidence, transparency, and trust in her as a mom.

Anabel's story is quite common in many African immigrant homes, where parents struggle to show affection because they didn't see their parents doing it. Their children, on the other hand, grow up in an affectionate culture. Nathan, a sixteen-year old high schooler, narrated a scenario that may resonate with most youth from immigrant homes. Nathan's father drops him at school and picks him up at the end of each day. He compares his cultural experience as his father drops him off at school to that of his friends.

My dad often drops me off at 7:45 a.m. As soon as I get out of the car, with my bag barely out, he drives off, because he is rushing to work. Once a while, he will say bye to me. Often, we hardly share eye contact. As I look around, I often see other kids, mostly my age, some of my classmates, who get out of their cars, while their parents patiently wait for them. Such parents would either blow a kiss to their children or wave. I can see the affection in their eyes.

These observations are frequent in most African immigrant families, where it seems parents and their youthful children do not have much to share. That is contrary to the experiences of most of their non-African colleagues.

Recently, I (Cynthia) had to attend a wedding out of the town. As I exited the airport and waited for my ride in the passenger pickup area, I sat on an empty bench. Several travelers were waiting as well. Among the lot, what caught my eye was a white teenager who may have been about eighteen. His mother and father were picking him up. They parked their car at the curb. As soon as they spotted him, his father immediately got out of the car, walked to meet him, and gave him a big, warm hug. Meanwhile, his mom was sitting in the passenger seat, watching them admiringly. The guy got into the car, positioning himself right behind his mom. Just when he got the chance to put his backpack down next to his seat, his mother turned around and gave him a hug and a kiss. I saw the car moving, and as it did, his parents were engaged in an intense conversation with him.

As I sat down on the bench, still waiting for my ride, I thought to myself, "*This is the kind of love every teenager desires.*" Children often want to be held, touched, and cuddled. As they grow up, they have a natural desire for such love in ways that will make sense to them. While it is understandable that immigrant parents may not have experienced much affection, in a society that is individualistic and self-seeking, they must realize that such emotional support is critical. It is essential to demonstrate love to your children in ways that they will understand. Besides, developmental challenges associated with race and self-esteem create a gap that can only be filled by consistent expression of authentic love. Such assertions are particularly needed for young girls who would need affection and hugs from, especially their fathers. Otherwise, they may seek love in the wrong places.

For the children of immigrant parents, a lack of affection could mean an absence of love. In our focus group discussions, we asked the youth to tell us how their parents expressed affection to them.

Ahhhh, are you referring to my mother or father? What? Never!

—Abeiku, seventeen years old

My mother pointed to her upbringing to explain the struggle she experiences in expressing affection to us. She said when she was a kid, there was never a word of love. So, I believe that is why she struggles to show us affection. I used to ask her if she loved me, and she wouldn't even smile like I existed.

—Eva, fifteen years old

Likewise, Emma, a fourteen-year-old high schooler remarked:

My mom never tells me that she loves me. I mean never, so I wonder if she does love me. She will not hug me or kiss me. I see my friends' parents show them so much affection, and it breaks my heart. I wish me and my mom or dad could do the same. One time, I wanted to take the initiative to show affection to my mom, hoping that she would respond. When I hugged her, she pushed me away, and when I told her I loved her, she asked me "Why?" Since then, I decided not to try again.

Emelia, who is a seventeen-year-old college freshman, explained that when she asked her mom whether she loves her, her mom said this to her, angrily:

Nonsense! If I didn't love you and your siblings, I wouldn't work so hard to get you all that you need: your books, food to eat, and clothes to wear. I do all that for you, and you can tell me that. You people are so ungrateful. Go to Africa and see how people are suffering.

For the African immigrant parent, due to economic hardships in their countries of origin, the definition of love was the ability to provide for their daily needs. On the other hand, their children are growing in a culture where love implies something more than material things. In such cultures, food and material things abound, so providing for such needs may be considered necessities rather than a luxury. Besides, in Western culture, what young people need is mostly acceptance and affirmation. Simple statements from a parent to a child such as "You are so dear to me, I love you" or "See how pretty you look" could speak volumes on love to the youth.

In Western culture, parents spend a lot of time with their kids. They engage in activities such as going to the movies, attending their games, or going on vacations together. However, in the immigrant home, parents earn lower wages and must work multiple shifts to support their families here and back home, so such expectations become a challenge. Hence, even if they want to spend time with their children, they are severely limited. In the face of this reality, we encourage the youth to be more understanding when their parents' schedules are less accommodating and appreciate the little that they can do to demonstrate affection. At the same time, as a parent, you should understand the importance of being physically there for your children. If possible, this is where you may need to adjust your time commitments so that you apportion enough for your family. Such times will also enable you to instill godly counsel and guidance in the relationship. After all, your family remains your most significant treasure. The best way to protect this treasure is to give it quality time and nurturing. Parents must understand that money is not everything, "for where your treasure is, there your

> *In the face of this reality, we encourage the youth to be more understanding when their parents' schedules are less accommodating and appreciate the little that they can do to demonstrate affection.*

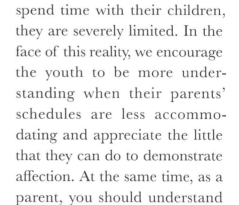

heart will be also" (Matt. 6:21). Most African immigrant parents work tirelessly so they can build huge houses in their home country, and some do that at the expense of investing time in their children. In as much as such investments are worthwhile, parents shouldn't prioritize these above the comfort and immediate wellbeing of their families. Often, such investments have turned into "ghost houses"; the owners hardly live in them. Psalm 127:3 further states that "Children are a heritage from the Lord, offspring a reward from him." Parents must preserve and nurture this treasure and heritage in love and godly discipline.

Discipline and Yelling

Every parent tries to raise their children in the best possible way. Regardless of how they train their children, they will misbehave at times. Parents may use a variety of strategies, some of which may have the intended effect of decreasing children's subsequent misbehavior. Generally, regardless of ethnic background, parents may use reasoning, yelling, or corporal punishment to discipline their children.

In as much as such investments are worthwhile, parents shouldn't prioritize these above the comfort and immediate wellbeing of their families.

Discipline in the African immigrant home is carried out differently from homes in Western culture. For instance, in a typical middle-income Caucasian home in the Western culture, a parent may use encouragement, timeouts, and loss of privileges to instill discipline. Assuming a child misbehaves in public, his or her parent(s) could plead or negotiate with them to stop: *"Bobby, please . . . stop it . . . you will get a timeout when we get home . . . no more video games for you, mister."* In the

African home, a parent may use a more confrontational and direct approach to discipline, such as yelling or some form of spanking. Alternatively, they may use a facial expression that the child understands to express displeasure at his or her misbehavior. The typical African thought is that if you spare the rod, you spoil the child, as Proverbs 13:24 indicates: "Whoever spares the rod hates their children, but the one who loves their children is careful to discipline them." African parents may, therefore, sometimes resort to physical punishment to instill the necessary discipline.

In our interview with the youth, one dominant theme that emerged as a form of discipline was yelling and insults.

> *They always yell and scream and insult you at the least provocation. So, you can't go to them for anything or talk to them apart from materialistic things or only education.*

> —*Eva, fifteen years-old*

For fear of being beaten, the child may look on and try to suppress their reactions because any unwanted attitude may attract a harsher punishment from his or her parent(s). Sixteen-year-old Abby narrates her experience:

> *"I've yelled before, and it resulted in me getting beaten, so ever since then, I stand there and let them scream, and when they're done, I go to my room."*

Some immigrant parents may resort to physical forms of punishment because, in their countries of origin, such types of punishment are common and acceptable. Immigrant parents transfer the same mindset to their new environment. However, Western culture does not support the physical exertion of pain, even if the goal is to correct. Experts advise against corporal punishment because it could model aggression, create shame and it is proven to be an ineffective form of discipline. The limits that the new culture sets on the choice of discipline may frustrate some parents and undermine their parental authority.

The use of spanking is not unique to African homes. Other homes in the Western world also use it, but the approach may differ. We will not be quick to prescribe a kind of discipline here. Every home is different, and each may call for a specific, rather than a prescribed way of handling a child. What we strive to accomplish is to throw light on the extent to which the immigrant culture has influenced the disciplinary approach that immigrant parents use in the West. Such information will help them to adjust their disciplinary strategies within their cultural context and to understand the disciplinary implications of whatever path they choose to use. Second, we amplify the difference between discipline and abuse.

Prov. 13:24: "Whoever spares the rod hates their children, but the one who loves their children is careful to discipline them", has been interpreted differently. The *rod* in this scripture could suggest a literal rod or a metaphorical rod. Either way, the goal of *the rod* is to direct, guide, and correct—not to harm. Training is done in love to produce the desired result. From Proverbs 22:6, parents, particularly Christians, are expected to raise their kids in the right way. There are two parts to this scripture: the training and the results. The training takes different forms, which in some homes may include the use of physical punishment. The other side deals with outcomes, such as good behaviors.

Eva, a fifteen-year-old added:

> *Spanking doesn't do anything to me; it just makes me hate you. What I will prefer is for me to dialogue with my mom or my dad, but especially my mom, because I am a girl. I want them to hear me out, and then they can let me know what they think. Sometimes, they spank without you knowing or understanding*

what you did, like for real. So, if my mom wanted me to clean the dishes and she beats me, it could be that the reason why I couldn't do the dishes was that I was studying for my math test, and I could have done it after. So, I get confused, and I am like, if I get bad grades, you will be mad and yell, and if I am not able to do the dishes because I was studying for my test, you will spank me. So, what should I do? Sometimes, they just need to breathe and talk, rather than just jump on me at the least issue.

As an immigrant parent, the outcomes you get from disciplining your child strongly depends on the type and nature of the discipline. Factors such as love, understanding, and empathy play a significant role in this training process. Regardless of the form of punishment, in Ephesians 6:4, parents are to refrain from provoking their children to anger, and they are to demonstrate unconditional love in their disciplinary efforts. A forceful disciplinary measure would not necessarily straighten out your child. What is more important is using the right disciplinary approach to get the right results. To accomplish this, we highlight the need to understand, first and foremost, your identity in this world. You are a Christian, and the Bible is your guide and final authority in all matters of life. Second, as immigrants, parenting will be more

To both parents and the youth, because the immigrant home has values from both the African and the Western culture, you should refrain from choosing one cultural world over the other.

natural in a new environment if you find ways to educate yourself on the rules of the host country. You must be careful not to allow your cultural practices to violate any aspect of the laws in the host country.

To our young people, you may need to adjust your actions and reactions to strike a balance between the African culture and the Western culture. God did not make a mistake by placing you in an African immigrant home. With its values on self-control, selflessness, community, humility, and character, your African heritage has so much to offer you. You would, however, need to patiently shift your mindset into becoming more patient with your parents. Learn to embrace some of the positive elements in their culture. You may see your friends talk back in a somewhat rebellious manner to their parents, but that should not be your standard. Even in mainstream Western culture, such behaviors are generally not acceptable. You must understand that discipline is necessary for correction.

To both parents and the youth, because the immigrant home has values from both the African and the Western culture, you should refrain from choosing one cultural world over the other. Remember, there are values and norms in both cultures that carry both positive and negative impacts on people. Such exposure will enable you to find the positive aspects of both cultures on issues of not just discipline, but choices, ways of living, and future ambitions. This approach to life embraces both cultures and produces a holistic upbringing for the youth.

CHAPTER THREE

I WANT THE BEST FOR YOU | DON'T LIVE YOUR LIFE THROUGH ME

Teenagers and young people in general, especially middle and older adolescents, are doing some serious thinking- about life, their values, and their faith. They are trying to make sense of what they have heard since they were children, and life has to make sense to them. —*Wayne Rice.*

God is full of love. He abounds in steadfast love to all who call on him (Ps. 86:5). God has placed a similar affection in the hearts of every parent towards their children and wired them with a burden to ensure their children succeed in life. Out of the same love, most immigrant parents have toiled tirelessly, maneuvering between multiple jobs to make a decent living for their families. Because of these challenges, they expect their children to listen to them and follow their instructions. Often, when this does not happen, it leaves parents frustrated. By contrast, Western culture teaches young ones to be assertive, and in some cases, their wishes may override that of older people.

Joel is a fifteen-year-old boy with Ghanaian parents. He had a casual chat with his friend, Jason. Jason's mom is Irish, and his dad is American. Joel and Jason often take the bus together, and Jason sometimes overhears conversations between Joel and his parents. He wonders if Joel's parents ever grant him his wishes. One sunny Friday afternoon, they both decided not to take the bus and instead join their friends at a nearby Starbucks. Right after school was over, Joel receives a call from his dad to take the bus. Not knowing how to communicate his disappointment to his friend, Joel just told Jason, *"I will see you on Monday."* Then, sadly, he hopped into the bus. The two friends texted a lot over the weekend. Still, Joel refused to talk about the situation. He didn't want his friend to see him as weak. On Monday, when they were back in school, Jason kept bugging him about why he can't step up to his parents. At lunchtime, as they sat in the cafeteria to eat, Jason broke the ice.

"Hey Joel, what do you do if your parents don't agree with you on something you want to do?"

"I didn't want to talk about this because it's so frustrating, Joel chimed in.

"My parents don't get it that we are not in Africa. They usually consider it disrespectful if I speak my mind on issues. Last Friday, my dad called me about not going to Starbucks, and I'm not supposed to talk back. That's why I didn't come with you." Joel pauses for a bit and bows down his head. He then continues, reluctantly.

"He wanted me to come home right after school . . . ermmm . . . since he said he didn't want me to get into a bad company. The pressure is too much. He has been pestering me to become a doctor because that is what he wanted to do but

couldn't pursue it due to financial constraints. I don't have any breathing space at home because he is always on my neck. He feels the wrong company could ruin this dream. Honestly, I want to be who I want to be and not who he thinks I should become."

"Sorry, you feel this way, Joel." Jason taps Joel on his back. *"So, what are you going to do about it?"* Jason quizzed.

"Well, I'd live with it till I leave for college, then they won't bother me anymore. I get to decide what I want to do when I am out of that house. I'm going to go to college far away."

"Wow, this is sad, Joel. You will be okay. Let's get out of here."

Sadly enough, many young people feel their parents' culture silences them and stifles their potential. These young people have their unique gifts, and they seek for avenues to develop them. They need an environment that will give them a voice and nurture their tender giftings. They are whispering to their parents, *"You can't live your life through me."*

Parental Passion

African immigrant parents are passionate about passing their cultural values on to their children. However, they could express this passion in ways that their children may completely misunderstand. Culture is dynamic. What you consider to be right for your child may have changed with the times. In our conversation with a Nigerian family, the mother narrated to us how she reacted to her sixteen-year-old daughter who wanted to go out with her friends and would return at 12:00 a.m.:

"When I was your age, I dared not go out like that with people my parents didn't know. They trained me to return home before 7:00 p.m. every day. Agreeing to return before 10:00 p.m. is the only way I am going to let you go."

Chidi, her daughter, who was frustrated and found this expectation absurd, responded to the mom in an angry tone:

"But mom, you want to enforce the rules that your parents used on you on me. This is 2018, and things are different. I know you love me and want the best for me, but it's a different generation, the times have changed. You always make me look weird among my friends because I can't do a lot of stuff that all of them can do. If you want the best for me as you say all the time, then can you please let me be free a bit? I know how to take care of myself, and I will be okay."

Her mom got furious. Out of anger, she refused to let Chidi go out. For the rest of the day, Chidi went to her room as usual and shut the door.

A related incident occurred when we visited a family to resolve a conflict between a dad and his seventeen-year-old son. The father repeatedly told his son: *"I am struggling in this country because of you. I don't need anything from you. I want it to be well with you, yet you don't listen to me."*

As a parent, it is natural to desire the best for your children. However, it might help if you express love and care in ways that are culturally relevant and understandable, not necessarily according to their understanding of love. Parents should learn to communicate the appropriate kind of love for their children based on their age, gender, and temperaments. That will go a long way to help foster a lasting, loving relationship between both parties, especially as their children grow and strive for independence and autonomy.

Some Things Change as We Grow

As young people grow, their craving for power and control increases. Nothing is more important to an adolescent than the acquisition of power and autonomy.[14] Autonomy has a special meaning during these years. It signifies the uniqueness, capability, and independence of a young person who wants to depend less on parents and other adults. At this stage, the youth expect their parents to give them some space and respect.[15]

Meanwhile, the African culture within which their parents grew up has little provision for such demands. With the African culture, often parents instruct their kids and expect them to do as they say. Talking back or questioning is unacceptable. These cultural dynamics play out in Tony's home:

> *"Tony, I told you to clean your room; why isn't it done?"*
> Tony's father mutters as he approaches Tony's room.

> *"Dad, I did it."*

> *"But it's just as dirty as it was."* At this point, Tony's father is in the room. His eyes lazily roam around the room. *"Look at your closet and the floor."*

> *"No, it isn't. I cleaned a bit. I plan to clean a bit more later,"* Tony responds, without lifting his eyes to look at his father.

"I want you to clean your room right now, no excuses. You always say you will do it later, and it never gets done."

"But I already did."

"You have a response to everything. Either you clean your room now, or you know what's going to happen."

[Silence]

"You won't mind me? Who do you think you are?"

[Silence]

What do we see playing out here? Control! Power! Tony wants to have a little control. Dad, on the other hand, asserts his role as the authority figure in the home. Even though some teens may delay in doing chores due to laziness, here, its clear Tony is not acting lazily. Instead, he is requesting dialogue and negotiation. In relating to adults, youth want to be influenced more by relationships than by power. They want to see their parents training them in love instead of responding to a set of unreasonable rules. In Ephesians 6:4, the amplified version explains this clearly: "Fathers, do not provoke your children to anger [do not exasperate them to the point of resentment with demands that are trivial or unreasonable or humiliating or abusive; nor by showing favoritism or indifference to any of them], but bring them up [tenderly, with lovingkindness] in the discipline and instruction of the Lord." The passage implies that parents can upset their children if they place unreasonable expectations on them.

Reasonable expectations have different meanings across cultures. In the Western context, the command to "train up a child in the way he should go" suggests you should not subject your children to unreasonable expectations, which means the training should involve a loving dialogue. With the conversation between Tony and his father, what he probably wanted to communicate to his father was, *"I know I should clean my room, but can I do it when I finish with what I am doing? I'm not you, Dad. I want to be myself. I feel that so long as I do it, the timing doesn't necessarily have to be on your terms. I may have more urgent things to attend to that you may not know."* But Tony struggles to put his thoughts across because his father would consider such a response as rude.

Parents must realize that their Western-born or raised children live in a culture that promotes individualism and autonomy. It is a culture that supports self-assertion. What these children are crying for is not total independence. They are only asking for a voice and a say. They want a little bit of some of the power that their parents have. After all, young people also have something to offer.

At his tender age, David trusted in God's ability to defeat Goliath while Saul, who was older, shuddered under Goliath's threats (1 Sam. 17). In *Myth or Mystery*, a 'bio-autobiography' of Apostle Professor Opoku Onyinah, the authors, Opoku Onyinah and Gibson Annor-Antwi demonstrate how young ones can be a channel or a voice through which God can speak to older people. In this book, an angel delivered a compelling message to a pastor through a teen girl. Initially, the pastor wondered why God wouldn't talk to him instead. Eventually, the encounter with the girl "left him one profound lesson–teamwork!"[16] The lesson from this story stresses how important it is for older people, including parents, to place a higher premium on what their children have to offer, rather than assuming they don't know much.

Conflicts arise when immigrant parents refuse to share some of their power with their children. In many immigrant homes, power struggles are frequent, and parents are quick to tell their children with the slightest display of self-assertion: "You will do what I tell you to do in this house. I am the parent—either you take it or leave it." Unfortunately, homes that act like this and exhibit minimal compromise and negotiation go through broken relationships, pain, and conflict.

As parents, know that one day your children will leave home. You have a limited time to spend with them. The question is, what will be their fond memories? Will the memories be love or silence, pain, and broken relationships? You must use the brief period you have to build good relationships; this will always pull your children back to you, even when they leave home. Otherwise, they will leave home for college or whatever reason and be reluctant to return. The last thing you would want to experience is losing your children to the dictates of the sophisticated anti-Christian system.

The need to foster good relationships in the immigrant home does not rest only with parents. You might be reading this book as a young lady or gentleman from an immigrant household. There is no doubt that you desire to have a closely knit family where you can freely express your fears, joys, and expectations and enjoy a good relationship. Already, you deal with identity struggles in a multicultural world. You hope that the home you belong to will give you the love and support that you desire. However, the cultural tension at home makes your quest for a healthy parent-child relationship almost unachievable.

As a young person, you probably see your desires, aspirations, and worldviews as miles apart from those of your parents and wonder if these will ever harmonize.

As a young person, you probably see your desires, aspirations, and worldviews as miles apart from those of your parents and wonder if these will ever harmonize. The only way this blend can be possible is if both worlds create an interactive platform of understanding.

In striving for such understanding, African immigrant parents should also try to see things from the lenses of their children and allow them a little room to operate. On the other hand, their children must be willing to adjust their lenses, open up and increasingly collaborate with them. Such understanding is hard to achieve in most immigrant homes because while young people want to explore, their parents seek to control their freedom.

The Helicopter Culture

Young people want to explore. The desire to try something new can make parents anxious. A parent may look at his son and think, *"He is too young, and he doesn't know what he is doing. The world is tough and complicated, and he needs me to make those decisions for him."* Such fears are valid. However, as a parent, it is necessary to let go at some point. Sometimes, young people learn better when they can explore their options with the guidance of an adult, rather than when the parent tells them what to do. They may make some mistakes along the way, but this is part of human development.

Parents must be ready for these changes and must be willing to understand that the transition into adulthood means increasing assertion, individualism, and a desire for freedom.

Growth comes with changes, and this applies to the youth as well. Parents must be ready for these changes and must be willing to understand that the transition into adulthood means increasing assertion, individualism, and a desire for freedom. Hence, as a parent, you may have to lower your expectations to live your life through your children. Such an attitude will prevent unnecessary stresses and foster cordial relationships.

We have a family friend with grown-up children who are all married. This family just can't let go. They want to determine where the children should live and how many children they should have. They want to decide on their career changes and other issues that concern them. As parents, you might not have been comfortable if your parents continued to press you to follow their wishes and plans. Likewise, you must get to that point where you adjust your expectations to acknowledge the development and growth of your children.

In Luke 2:41-52, the child Jesus at the tender age of twelve exercised some assertion. His parents were looking for him. "When his parents saw him, they were astonished. His mother said to him, 'Son, why have you treated us like this? Your father and I have been anxiously searching for you.'" Jesus replied, "Why were you searching for me…..?" At this point, Jesus was pursuing his God-given agenda. He was seeking knowledge about his mission on earth before he launched out, so He wondered why his parents would track him down. We acknowledge that twelve years old is too early for independence. Nonetheless, it is necessary to have a certain reasonable level of autonomy and assertion at any age. Like the child Jesus, your young children may resist the tendency to embrace all your wishes because consciously or unconsciously, they are preparing for adulthood. They are busy equipping themselves with the tools that they will need when they are older. These life skills are necessary for decision making, learning, relating, taking responsibility, and other virtues of adult life. When they begin to emerge with these kinds of growth indicators, it may become naturally tricky for the average African parent to accept. Parents, therefore, might want to consider adjusting a few areas as far as relating to and releasing their children are concerned. It is a prerequisite for self-development and maturity.

"Just Do It for Me" Syndrome

In our ministering to the youth, we have encountered several young people who feel they are living for their parents. Such people either choose a career to please their father or marry that person to make the mother happy. Many of these young ones have hinted, *"I did it to make my daddy happy. He wanted me to do this."* That is an unfortunate reality. One young man told me (George), *"I became a pharmacist because my parents wanted me to do it so badly. The pressure was way too much. But now, I am back in school because after I practiced for a few years, I realized pharmacy was not for me, so I am in the middle of switching careers. I am so mad at my parents now because I feel they have wasted my time."*

Abeo, who is originally from Nigeria, repeatedly tells the father who believes medicine is best for him that he does not like it. He explains: *"My father is forcing me to become a medical doctor, but I am not born for it. I can't stand blood. I don't think I am going to last in that field if I go that route."* Abeo's dad's rationale for pushing the son into medicine is because he is a medical doctor himself, and he has a clinic in Nigeria. He hopes that one day Abeo would relocate to Nigeria to oversee his medical practice. Abeo, however, thinks differently. *"I love to read, and I love to analyze cases. I believe it would be best if I were to become an attorney."* Abeo tries to tell his father: *"You cannot live your life through me."* Yet, the father doesn't budge.

The reason why some immigrant parents may compel their children into specific careers may be economic or social. The rationale is often to ensure that these children have a secure future. Most of the medical and legal fields such as medicine, nursing, pharmacy, and law have six-figure salaries. Hence, parents assume that regardless of passion, going into such jobs will ensure a good income. Sometimes, as immigrant parents, we are so quick to make statements like:

"Look at your cousin, she chose to become a nurse, and today she is making it and can cater for the family. You look at the car she drives."

"Look at Kwame: he went to Yale University, and now he has become wealthy. Most companies want him. I want you, my son, also to go to Yale and take the path that Kwame did so you can become successful like Kwame. Just do it for me."

A career is a lifelong endeavor so the monetary factor may be necessary. Still, it should not drive all that we do. The reality is that some in the medical field will eventually quit. The problem with pushing your child into the wrong career is that you may be attacking the identity of that child, and second, you may be killing his or her drive. Your child is not a photocopy of another person. God created them as one of a kind with a carved-out path to success and not to be like someone else.

> *Your child is not a photocopy of another person. God created them as one of a kind with a carved-out path to success and not to be like someone else.*

In some cases, your child may be wired for the art field and could excel as an artist or a journalist instead of as a doctor or lawyer. When compelled to become a nurse, such a person loses their identity as an artist and battles the concept of becoming who they are not. Wearing the uniform could make the person look like someone else. Your child may go to Yale University and do the same major as Kwame did but would fail to succeed if that is not what God has destined for them. God's will is always the best for our children.

We humbly admonish that parents should not force their children to have the same identity or ambition as them, a friend, or

We humbly admonish that parents should not force their children to have the same identity or ambition as them, a friend, or someone the parents admire.

someone the parents admire. They should, however, guide their children in identifying, discovering, and pursuing their God-given path. Demanding that they *"just do it for you"* would only leave them desperate and frustrated; allow them to find their own identity. You do not want to satisfy yourself temporarily and leave them with the permanent mark of unfulfilled dreams. If you keep pressuring them this way, you could stifle their potential, or they may eventually rebel in the fight for their identity. It is like a captive who is fighting for freedom; either he gives up or rebels.

The *"just do it for me"* syndrome also applies to relationships. In some immigrant homes, parents may compel their young adults to marry a man or a woman who they think is ideal. On the other hand, your children may want to make that decision. Rose, a mother of three teenage girls, intimated to us:

> *It's fascinating to see the kind of boys our kids are marrying today. If you are not careful, they will go and bring some boy with a crazy hairstyle. You wonder how such boys can be good*

*husbands, and if you tell them the type of men to marry, they
don't want to listen.*

Here, Rose needs to realize that the times have changed, and,
in this culture, fancy haircuts may not necessarily mean that a gentleman is bad or irresponsible. Rather than imposing your preferences on your children, we suggest that you use godly principles
and love to guide them in such decisions. You can collaboratively
do this rather than sounding imposing or intimidating.

Young people must also know that in such situations and decision-making processes, your parents are not always wrong. Marriage
is marriage; the terms and procedures may have changed with the
times, but the core principles of choosing the right partner and
having a successful marriage remain the same, so your parent's
views remain relevant. Even though the way they communicate
such knowledge may be hard to understand, the content might
be worth your attention. Instead of seeing them as old fashioned,
appreciate their experience and wisdom. Know that parents are a
blessing from the Lord; God gives them to you for a purpose. If you
collaborate with them and glean from their wisdom and experience,
it can help you avoid some costly mistakes.

Becoming Me and Maintaining Us

Young people desire to be assertive and different from everyone
else. This mindset, however, may seem outrageous to your parents as they seek to "parent" you. The reality is you live in two
worlds! These are two worlds with different worldviews; whereas
one desires freedom, the other wants to dominate. Immigrant parents and their children predominantly affiliate more with one of
these worlds. The only way they can avoid conflict is when they find
a common ground in these two conflicting worlds. Young people
must accommodate the views of their parents as they navigate the

journey of *becoming you.* You can "become you" without hurting their feelings or engaging them in conflict.

As a young person, there are many things you can learn from your parents without stifling your sense of identity. Assume that you want a new phone and ask your parents to get you one. Your father may snarl, *"You have a phone. I don't have any money to get you another phone."* Anytime you bring up the conversation, you may get the same response. Your mother, on the other hand, ignores you as if you do not exist. This response can frustrate you because all your friends have the kind of phone you want. So, besides your phone not working, probably you want this phone model to enable you to fit in with your peers. As a youth, you may face such a situation or a similar one. But how do you react in such instances, such that you end up possibly getting what you want without causing any conflict? You could get some inner prompts to respond angrily and probably tell them that *"If you don't get it for me, I know how to get it myself."* But you hear another still small voice saying, *"Don't go that route; just be patient."* Which voice will you follow? Sometimes, for the sake of peace, you just must let go. As a young person, make every effort not to let "self" override your need to honor your caretakers. If you are patient and adopt a more positive and respectful posture, you may end up getting what you want.

Transition into adulthood comes with an instinct for self-assertion. A test of real growth and maturity, though, is how you manage that craving for independence against your parents' need to feel respected in your growth process. You do have a critical responsibility to grow into the person God wants you to become, without breaking the boundaries of honor for your parents and spiritual shepherds.

Some young people try to assert themselves wrongly by smoking and drinking to demonstrate their independence from parents and religious establishments. Others begin to engage in premarital sexual relationships to portray their freedom from the so-called ethical rules. These are false ways of attempting to express one's identity. Youth, know who you are. God did not create you to get hooked on drugs and to fulfill the lustful desires of the flesh. Instead, you exist to please God with your life. It's the only expression that can give you real meaning and fulfillment. Any engagements or activity that takes you outside of the holy standards of God's word will lead you into becoming who you are not.

As you grow into *becoming you*, you need the guidance of your parents. Besides that, your reference manual for life is all written in the Bible. The Bible can guide you in this dark and morally conflicting world. In the Amplified version of scripture, the Bible instructs us to "remove not the ancient landmark which your fathers have set up" (Prov. 22:28). The original landmarks of the Israelites were essential methods of identifying each person's land, as the inheritance passed down from one generation to another. No one was to remove these landmarks (Deut. 19:14). Likewise, in our lives, we should not dismiss the markers of holy living and humility. We should seek to preserve the prominent scriptural landmarks such as a life of prayer, moral values, decent Christian dressing, and pursuit of intimacy with God. The Bible presents us with several tenets and sound

Becoming the real you, therefore, does not mean rebelling. Neither does it mean being arrogant. What it means is "being you" and respecting and maintaining the "us" that binds the family together.

doctrines to help us maneuver our lives in this changing world. God never changes, and his Word doesn't change either. The world, with its beliefs, standards, pleasures, and culture will pass away, but the Word of God will remain forever (Luke 21:33). If we build our lives on the Word, it assures us of longevity and security.

Yes, there is a need for self-expression, but as a young person, you should always ask yourself when you have a decision to make: "*Is this what God wants for me? Does this present a real image of my identity in Christ? Does this character or this attitude portray me as an authentic representative of the Lord Jesus Christ?*" See how the Apostle Peter describes you: "But you are a chosen people, a royal priesthood, a holy nation, God's special possession, that you may declare the praises of him who called you out of darkness into his wonderful light" (1 Pet. 2:9). Becoming the real you, therefore, does not mean rebelling. Neither does it mean being arrogant. What it means is "*being you*" and respecting and maintaining the "*us*" that binds the family together.

---- CHAPTER FOUR ----

MY CHILD DOESN'T UNDERSTAND ME | MY PARENTS DON'T GET IT | WE ALL DON'T GET IT

Tolerance and celebration of individual differences is the fire that fuels lasting love.—*Tom Hannah*

It is one Saturday afternoon in late spring. Forty-five-year-old Mrs. Ekuful sits on her patio, relaxing. Sipping a glass of orange juice, she chats hysterically on the phone with her sister in Ghana. Her voice radiates through the neighborhood. While still talking, she opens the sliding door, which connects the patio to the kitchen and yells out her daughter's name.

"Abena!"

"Abena! How many times should I call you before you respond?"
Mrs. Ekuful walks to the kitchen.

Abena comes out of her room towards the kitchen, holding her phone. *"Mommy, I didn't hear you call. I was in my room."*

"Do I have water in my mouth? What were you doing in that room? Get off that stupid phone. Can that phone give you

food to eat? Haven't I told you repeatedly that you need to do the dishes? And you haven't even bathed your brother all day. Why are you so stubborn? Do you even understand when I speak? You are lucky; do you know how much work I had to do when I came back from school when I was in Ghana? Go to Ghana and see."

Abena shrugs and rolls her eyes, feeling exhausted emotionally by her mother's rambling. *"Mom, please. I wasn't on my phone."*

Abena stands in the kitchen but keeps a distance from her mother. Mrs. Ekuful walks to the sink to drop her glass.

"Be quiet! I would have given you a dirty slap if you were close to me. Nonsense! How dare you shut me up. Who do you think you are? America is getting to your head. I will not tolerate this craziness at my house."

Mrs. Ekuful walks towards Abena.

"Get out of my face and go do what I asked you to do before I get angry."

"Mom, please, I was finishing up my project. I have two different projects due next week, and I was trying to get through one of them, and then I will do the dishes."

"Are you to tell me what to do? Get out of my face."

[Abena walks away silently with a frowned face to do the dishes.]

If you are to see through the living room window of an immigrant family, you will possibly see a similar exchange like the one between Abena and her mom. Most African immigrant households show two cultural worlds, with varying shades. The differences depend on how much the parents have adjusted to Western culture. It also depends on how children have adapted to their parents' culture.

Abena is a sixteen-year-old high schooler who was born and raised in the United States. She is the oldest of three children. This Saturday, she does what she thinks are her chores and then takes a bit of time to catch up with her schoolwork. She prepares breakfast for her two siblings, does the laundry, and cleans the bathrooms. She does not want her siblings to disturb her, so she goes to her room to work on her school project. Meanwhile, she turns the TV channel to Disney to engage them. At 1:00 p.m., she returns to the kitchen to make lunch for them. The sink is full of dishes at this point, but she thought to herself, *"This can wait."* All the while, Abena's mom, who works an overnight shift, was sleeping. She wakes up at 1:45 p.m., gets something to eat, and decides to relax in the backyard. Abena is nowhere in the living area; she knew she was in her room and assumes that she is on her phone. So, when she decides to call Abena out, she is already furious.

Such exchanges in African immigrant homes occur because

> *The tension with responsibilities in immigrant homes gets worse when parents fail to acknowledge their children for doing the right thing but highlight their wrongdoing.*

parents may not completely understand the struggles their children go through. Some parents do not know the amount of homework their children have to do every day because as they grew up in

Africa, they didn't have to do as much homework as it is in today's culture. Young people often have other responsibilities such as homework and other projects that they must work on besides doing chores at home. For middle schoolers, high schoolers, and college students, these responsibilities could extend into the weekend.

The youth believe parents must allow them to invest much of their energy in their education. They feel it is unfair for parents to expect them to do most of the house chores since their peers do not have to live by such standards. The tension with responsibilities in immigrant homes gets worse when parents fail to acknowledge their children for doing the right thing but highlight their wrongdoing. In Abena and her mom's story, her mom did not bother to recognize that Abena had fed her siblings, done the laundry, and cleaned the bathrooms, and so Abena felt unappreciated. The undue responsibilities immigrant parents put on their children make some think that doing house chores is more important to their parents than excelling in school. So they get more confused when, despite the pressure at home, parents expect them to make all A's in their classes.

> *Ironically, it is the same African culture that draws the line of conflict and misunderstanding between the two generations.*

The youth from African immigrant homes describe the culture of their parents—African, which is vastly different from what they see as their culture. Interestingly, they do not associate themselves with the American culture, per se. Instead, they identify their own culture—what we have termed the *"youth African and American*

subculture". Their culture is not entirely African or American but just a youthful culture. This culture has a bit of the American or Western culture and the African culture, plus the culture defined by their generation.

Children of African immigrant parents do not necessarily prefer Western culture over the African culture. Many of them lean more towards African culture in many ways. However, the youth subculture, which is mostly shaped by Western culture, has a global reach. Hence, people see it as aligning more with Western culture than the African culture. In reality, children of immigrant parents, who are born or raised in the West are Africans at heart.

In the focus group, as the youth expressed the differences between their (youth) culture and that of their parents, we inquired if they wished their parents were more Americanized. Here's how Esi responded:

> *I don't think we want them to change to become Americans because we understand they didn't grow up here. And, we like the fact that the African culture is unique, and we want to keep that. But we wish they are more understanding of the complex cultures of the two worlds we have to deal with. Since we were born here, it is kind of like we take bits and pieces of both worlds. So, we end up doing some stuff that may be more American, and that may be a problem for them.*

> *—Esi, sixteen years old*

Most youth appreciate their African roots and, for that matter, their parents' culture. Ironically, it is the same African culture that draws the line of conflict and misunderstanding between the two generations. We see such tension in phrases and expressions from the youth such as "they don't get it," "my mom is too extra," "I just can't deal with them," "I can't relate to my parents," and "They don't understand my world." Just as they appreciate their parents' roots, the youth also expect their parents to be more open to their cultural world. However, parents may be frustrated because they feel their children rather don't understand their views. Phrases such as, "Why can't you understand me," "I have been your age before, and I know better than you do," or "You just don't respect" demonstrate such emotions. Therefore, is it an issue of "We all don't get it, rather than "My mom or my child doesn't get it?"

Anthony E. Wolf's book *I'd Listen to My Parents if They'd Just Shut Up* explains the relationship dynamics between parents and their children.[17] Though the title of this book may sound harsh for the average African parent, we think we can glean some ideas from it. As we wrote this book, we reflected on Wolf's views. We wondered whether the conflict between immigrant parents and their children is due to a lack of communication. Wolf's position is that sometimes parents need to allow their children to talk instead of driving the conversation from their prejudices. King Solomon cleverly crafts this point in Proverbs 14:29: "Whoever is patient has great understanding but one who is quick-tempered displays folly." Solomon's wise counsel suggests that there is wisdom and understanding in listening.

It is reassuring to the youth to see that their parents are actively listening in as they speak. I (George) have had instances where my ten-year-old daughter would say, "Daddy listen. I am talking to you; can you listen to me?" I decided to give her my full attention. Parents should not be distracted or multitasking during essential conversations. As parents, when you listen, you appropriately interject without being overly intrusive. This strategy will ensure that your child fully expresses his or her thoughts and opinions. Wolf further suggests that, if necessary, parents should wait to discuss sensitive issues later. They should refrain from providing a long lecture that could stifle the communication line, since there is a time for everything (Eccl. 3:1).

Let's Talk

Communication is the "exchange of thoughts, messages, or information, through speech, signals, writing, or behavior."[18] Biblical communication is a two-way street of sharing or reasoning together (Isa. 1:18a). Effective communication builds emotional ties and enhances mutual understanding. Dale Carnegie's statement, "You can make more friends in two weeks by becoming a good listener than you can in two years trying to get other people interested in you,"[19] demonstrates the importance of effective communication through listening. Effective communication is more vital in immigrant homes, where there is a higher tendency for misunderstandings because of the presence of two cultures.

In the Bible, communication is sharing and fellowship. Such conversation must focus on *talking with,* rather than *talking to.* The *talking with* style somehow mimics the communication style of Western culture, which upholds the expression of views, regardless of age. However, in the African immigrant home, the *talking to* style is more common. When you enter a typical African home, you will observe parents giving instructions to their children, who usually don't respond much.

African parenting structure for the most part defines the relationship between parents and children in hierarchical terms. Hence, the communication style takes a top-down approach. There usually is little room to consider the child's opinion. Parents may feel insulted when people younger than they talk to them in a culturally unacceptable manner. Onwujuba and Marks describe Nigerian immigrants' parenting in the United States.[20] They stress that in Nigeria, like most African countries, parenting is deemed a near-sacred role. In such cultures, parents expect children to defer to the adult on most decision. Parents have absolute power to raise their children in ways that they deem fit. However, they note further that the Nigerian parents who have migrated to the United States have had to change their communication styles. In Western culture, the children have grown up in school systems and environments that guarantee them the right to speak.

Parents raising their children in such situations must remember that their understanding of communication is different from how their children see it. For children, communication is sharing of core values. Values are the core principles of a society or people. One essential purpose of parental communication is to pass on cultural values to the next generation. Growing up, African parents have learned Christian and family cultural principles. For them to pass on these cherished values to their children, the family should establish broad family principles that would bind both parents and children. For instance, for their children to respect their moral authority, parents must lead by example and live by those values.

So, what we put forth here is an approach that adopts the positive aspects of the various methods and compresses them into a whole communication package, tailored to the need of the individual child.

Proverbs 22:6 instructs that parents should "train up a child in the way he should grow so when he becomes old, he will not depart." The instruction is for immigrant parents to instill godly virtues, such as love, care, patience, morality, faith, discipline, and wisdom in the children, which will ensure positive results (Josh. 1:7–8). A significant way to effectively transfer such norms is through communication. This kind of communication should make sense to the younger

generation, which has both the communication styles of their parents' culture and the mainstream culture.

The question is, what type of communication strategies and methods should immigrant parents and their children adopt? How can both worlds adjust to the communication styles of the other? In answering this question, we don't aim to prescribe a specific approach since different parenting styles determine the nature of parent-child communication.[21] For instance, an authoritarian parent may adopt the more traditional way of parenting; this can instill discipline but potentially stifle parent-child conversations. On the other hand, a permissive parent may allow a child a lot of freedom to express themselves. The drawback is such a child could end up being unruly or undisciplined. In between these two extremes is the authoritative parent, who may communicate and explain household rules to their child in a respectful and warm but firm tone. Each parenting style has its setbacks. So, what we put forth here is an approach that adopts the positive aspects of the various methods and compresses them into a whole communication package, tailored to the need of the individual child.

As an African immigrant parent, you might be more comfortable with the authoritarian style of parenting. Again, this is where we caution you to improve your tolerance level. You can be both patient and firm if you desire to raise well-cultured and God-fearing children in the Western world, and you can do this without compromising your core cultural and biblical values.

A critical element in communication is tolerance and understanding. It is hard to understand someone without actively listening to what they have to say. Listening involves not being too quick to correct but waiting to do so at the right time. Proverbs 25:11 says, "A word fitly spoken is like apples of gold in a setting of silver." This scripture is a beautiful picture of the value of the right word spoken at the perfect time. Words do not only lift and encourage others, but they add value. They can be precious and more meaningful if we express them at the right moment.

Youth often want to talk to someone they can call a friend. They crave a sense of belonging. We advise parents to take advantage of this longing and create a platform for open and nonjudgmental conversations with their young ones. Most youth raised in African homes refrain from discussing certain things with their parents. They think they can't even have simple conversations about chores, school, and career without being judged wrongly. Hence, they are reluctant to disclose all their issues to their parents. Instead, they fake their real character. Some may prefer to confide in their peers. Others may choose to hold it in until they figure something out—unfortunately, those who cannot manage the pressure may end up hurting themselves or being hurt by others. Over the past years, we have counseled and prayed for several young people who are depressed or suicidal. For the most part, their main issue was they couldn't find an outlet or a listening ear for their challenges. There are many of our young people who carry smiles on their faces, but within them is an ongoing war. They cry within for mentors who would understand and stand with them in their pain and struggles. But often, there a few people, if any, who they can trust.

Regardless of the coping strategies the youth may use, the absence of parents in such emotional struggles leaves room for several adverse consequences. Seventeen-year-old Amos found himself at a drive-by shooting. He just happened to be there. Amos was fortunate enough not to be shot while he hid in a gas station. He narrated how he was so scared to call his mom or dad. When asked why, he laughed it off and commented:

> *My dad would have been furious at me that day. I am sure*
> *my parents wouldn't even let me complete my sentence on the*

phone if I told them there was a shooting. They would have started yelling and asked why I was there in the first place. They would have assumed I was possibly in the company of bad friends. Since I wasn't ready for the long lecture, I called my friend's dad to pick me up. Till today, my parents don't even know what went on.

This dramatic shooting incident can traumatize every observer. As young as he is, Amos was terrified by the shooting incident. Unfortunately, he couldn't share his experience with his parents to get the necessary emotional support. Like Amos, several young people raised in immigrant homes find themselves in such situations. They are often skeptical about discussing issues such as abuse, friends, choices, sexuality, their struggles as Blacks, and other sensitive topics with their parents. They feel their parents either misunderstand or misrepresent their sentiments on such issues. Immigrant parents must acquaint themselves with these struggles so that they know how to create a comfortable environment to enable effectual mutual communication. Using 1 Corinthians 13 as a benchmark, parents must be patient enough to listen and give their children the benefit of the doubt. It will go a long way to build relationships and confidence in such homes.

A study by the Associated Press and MTV interviewed 1,300 young people, with ages ranging between twelve and twenty-four. They found that most of these young people find the most happiness with family rather than friends. Most of the youth listed their parents as their heroes. The point is, children will always need emotional support, and they often search for this support at home. If they don't get it, they will find it elsewhere.[22] It falls on parents to create an enabling and nonjudgmental environment where their children can freely communicate their challenges, fears, and insecurities. It begins with healthy dialogue on the most trivial issues of the home, such as chores, school, or hygiene. The little conversations will then open the door for a discussion of their most complicated problems.

Can you imagine your child's joy if you begin to make time to playfully chat on the everyday things that interest them? How about discussing a game with your teen, or asking about their friends? We suggest that Christian parents should begin any dialogue on a positive note. They should also make sure that the timing is right. They can initiate discussions that portray care rather than querying. If you question your child on sensitive topics from the beginning of a conversation, they may fold up. As you give your child enough time to be comfortable, you can then express your concerns or the issues that need addressing. I (George) spoke to a lady who expressed a lot of frustration about how her parents are not interested in other aspects of her life. She believes she does not have a good relationship with them because they are boring; all they talk about is school and church. But she feels there is more to life than school and church (we discuss this further in Chapter 6). In talking with youth, the conversation should not cover only their education or church. You can engage them in other areas of their lives, such as sports, career, relationships, friendships, and racism.

The point is, children will always need emotional support, and they often search for this support at home. If they don't get it, they will find it elsewhere.

In a recent development of racism involving a Black man, George Floyd in Minneapolis, Minnesota, who was brutally killed by a White police officer, thousands of people, especially Black youth, were distraught. For most Black youth in immigrant homes, the sense of frustration was heightened due to the lack of openness and communication between them and their parents. While the young people wanted to be involved in activism against the racial injustices, parents took a more laid-back approach. They felt they needed time to process the events and also to resort to the power of prayer in handling the issue. The different responses to an issue that affects both generations were due to the varied cultural and generational backgrounds.

Immigrant parents who did not experience elementary education and were also not born in America have limited knowledge on American civic education and racial issues. Their children, on the other hand, experience and perceive racism as an average Black person would do due to their exposure. In the case of George Floyd's death, the difference in perception between parents and their children resulted in a lot of misunderstanding. This confusion could have been avoided if parents were more open to such discussions, and youth appreciated their parents' cultural posture. The more parents interact with their children, the stronger the parent-child relationship becomes. But this will not just happen; both youth and their parents must be intentional about this.

One other way to improve communication and understanding in immigrant homes is if families discuss cultural values and their respective meanings in both the African and Western cultures. Young people often get confused about how the meanings of cultural values differ across cultures. Onwujuba and Marks expressed their frustration on how the differences between the Nigerian and American culture confuse children of Nigerian immigrants living in the United States.[23] In Nigerian culture, a "no" means no. In Western culture, though, a "no" is often accompanied by "why." They explain that the tendency to question, or what some parents may consider "talking back," is a fallout of Western culture. Because their children have adapted to Western culture, their communication style reflects the same. However, these same children grow in homes with predominantly Nigerian culture. Hence, they have picked up the cultural values from both worlds. The child then has to switch between the two worlds, depending on where they are; at home, they are Nigerians, but when they leave the door, they become Americans. For instance, at home, a parent would expect their child to accept a "no" as a "no." At school, however, where the mainstream culture teaches self-assertiveness, it may be a different story. Switching between these worlds can be both difficult and confusing. Abena extensively explains the two worlds that she faces every day and how they confuse her:

> *At school, different shades of racism occur, but generally, no teacher yells at you. You can freely express yourself if you don't understand something. The teacher respects your opinion, whether they like you or not. Because even if they don't like you, they try to hide it for the most part. When I come home, it is a different story. My parents yell or spank. Sometimes, they call you names. For me, when you yell, I find it challenging to know what you are trying to tell me, so I end up ignoring you.*

Outside of the immigrant home, youth see their peers demonstrating a lot of assertiveness. This expression affects their communication styles and dilutes their African values on respect and honor. Such influences arouse tension in the home when parents disapprove of contrary values. Amid conflicting cultures and values, youth get confused as to what is acceptable. They wonder, to what extent should I be African or American? Where should I act all American or all African? They don't know. If parents expect them to know who to be at what time, what they are telling them is to figure out the conflicting values on their own. For most children, the result of such expectations is emotional stresses and psychological struggles.

African culture plays a significant role in the life of the youth whose parents are African immigrants. We suggest that it is okay for immigrant parents to continue instilling their cultural values into their children. However, they will have to consciously choose the more culturally approved parenting behaviors and attitudes of the host culture. They can then blend it with certain aspects of theirs. For instance, a parent can choose to maintain an Africa value of respect and honor, such as referring to an older person as "mom," "dad," "aunt," "uncle," and so on rather than calling them by their first names. However, within the same context of respect, they can modify the concept of "do as I say" to "let us reason together," (Isa. 1:18) but, of course, with the parent guiding the whole process.

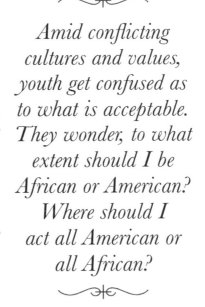

Amid conflicting cultures and values, youth get confused as to what is acceptable. They wonder, to what extent should I be African or American? Where should I act all American or all African?

Immigrant parents will need to understand that communication goes beyond talking to a child; it must be a two-way street. This approach doesn't mean the parent loses authority; neither does it mean the child assumes the leading role. What it suggests is that the parent is facilitating the conversation and creating a comfortable atmosphere in which the child can express themselves. Often, much of the yelling in African homes could be due to assumptions that parents may make about the actions or inactions of their children. Open communications discourage such wrong assumptions and misunderstandings.

As much as children hate yelling, no parent enjoys it either. Finding common ground to communicate in immigrant homes effectively will, therefore, relieve both parents and their children of the unwanted stress of ineffective communication. It will also require that in instances of conflict, children of immigrant parents do not demonstrate wrong attitudes towards their parents. Instead, they should realize that their parents are used to a certain level of parental authority, which seems to be diminishing within the Western context. Hence, both groups must demonstrate a lot of patience and tolerance as they strive for better communication. Improved communication will open the door for fruitful discussions on several issues, such as education and future goals.

Education and Careers

Africans, like most groups, believe in the importance of education. For instance, a proverb in Nigerian culture is that the best heritage to leave your children is not jewelry or material things but knowledge. Similarly, parents in other cultures, such as Ghana, firmly uphold education. Some immigrant parents may not have gotten the opportunity to get the best education. Hence, they try to push their children to take their education seriously. Children of immigrant parents often must deal with such high academic expectations and compete with peers who, for the most part, may not have the same level of expectations on

When the children raised in African immigrant homes do not receive a level of praise like what they see their friends get, they may think their parents don't appreciate them as much.

78

them. Hence, children may think that their parents are unfair to them since their colleagues are allowed to have a more laid-back life.

In the average African home, any grade below an *A* is often unacceptable! On the other hand, a colleague may be celebrating over a *B*. In most parts of the Western world, parents praise their children over the slightest accomplishment. We attended our son's kindergarten musical concert in 2019. What amazed us was how one parent brought flowers to present to her daughter for her music recital. I (Cynthia) dropped my jaw in disbelief! A whole bouquet for just a group kindergarten recital? Even though it might sound absurd for a typical African immigrant, the reality is this is the kind of society that the immigrant family lives in. It is a culture that rewards the slightest effort. Even though we have spelt out reward systems in our home, when we arrived home from the recital, our five-year-old son who participated in the concert and saw his friend getting the flowers whispered, "Am I going to get a prize?" We commended him again for a great job, and reminded him that as a family, we have our own way of rewarding him and his siblings. We then assured him that he would get his prize at the end of the school year if he does well.

When the children raised in African immigrant homes do not receive a level of praise like what they see their friends get, they may think their parents don't appreciate them as much. This feeling can be worse if parents approach such issues in a harsh and non-cooperative manner. In many of these instances, the reason why immigrant parents could decide not to praise their children overly is to set higher standards for them. But the only way parents can effectively communicate such good intentions is to use an approach that their children can understand. While high expectations have helped some young people to be high achievers, for others, it could be undesirable and discouraging. Some children prefer that their parents would reason with them a little bit, rather than thinking they are not working any harder. One immigrant child narrated how he does not receive the necessary support from home, yet his parents expect him to get all *A*'s in his class.

> *Both of my parents are not so educated. They can speak a little English and have no idea what I study in school. Sometimes, I need help with my homework or project, and they can't help me out. I resort to Google for help, but if I could get a human being to assist me at home, it would make a whole lot of a difference. I do the best I can. I compete with friends who receive enough help at home. Yet, when I make a B, I am scared to disclose it to them. Often, I hide my grades if I make anything below their expectation.*

> —*Josh, fifteen years old*

Sandra also expressed a similar sentiment. Even though she appreciates the fact that her parents care about her doing well, she wishes they would approach it in a more loving and understanding manner.

> *School is hard, and I think sometimes my parents don't get it. If I do well in a course, my mom acts like it is not a big deal. But if I make a grade that is below expectation, then she gets all mad. It upsets me a lot because it discourages me from working harder since there is no incentive to do so. I want my parents to reward me, or at least appreciate my efforts. Also, instead of yelling at me for not being serious, I think it will help to understand why I am struggling in that course.*

> —*Sandra, fourteen years old*

Related to the issue of education are career choices and preferences. Immigrant parents tend to have their specific career expectations for their children. Any child who goes against their preference may face their disapproval. Preferred jobs among immigrants include medicine, pharmacy, nursing, engineering, law, information technology, and such with lucrative incomes. Most immigrant parents have struggled through their stay abroad, doing menial jobs with meager salaries. They don't want their children to experience a similar trend. So, they push them into professional careers, which will provide them with a secure entrance into the job market later in life.

When the children raised in African immigrant homes do not receive a level of praise like what they see their friends get, they may think their parents don't appreciate them as much.

The pressure parents impose on their children on career choices has become a significant issue in many immigrant homes. Whereas parents opt for professions for their children, the children, on the other hand, who may have explored the opportunities available for them, may think otherwise. An immigrant child expressed that he feels that sometimes his parents want him to live the life that they didn't get to live.

> I was telling my mom that I wanted to do journalism the other time because I am very good at English, and I am a great speaker, and she said to me that "No! You are going to do nursing." I asked her if we could discuss it further, and she said, there is nothing to talk about; it is nursing or nothing, and she added, "Where are you going with that journalism?

—Michael, seventeen years old

Some immigrant parents are stuck with what they know as lucrative professions from their experiences in their respective home countries. They may not be so current with opportunities in the new environment, and what may be available for their children who were either born or raised in the West. Hence, it might be necessary for such parents to learn about other nontraditional careers such as manufacturing, sales, entrepreneurship, sports, music, arts, and investment. Several young people did not become medical doctors or engineers and yet have excelled in other fields of endeavor.

In dialogues with their parents, youth should also be reasonable with their expectations of what career to pursue. Young people must have the facts to prove why a specific profession is worth their time. Also, you should refrain from choosing careers just because you want to explore, or because it is trendy. Instead, strive to pursue jobs that match your passion and skills, and that would provide a decent income, so you don't become a burden on your parents in the future. This position will create a mutual understanding between parents and children and minimize the unnecessary conflict in such choices.

Food and Chores

Immigrant parents love their ethnic cuisine. As a parent, you may have known these dishes all your life, so it is hard to adjust to the Western dishes. In most African immigrant homes, families cook food from scratch. On the other hand, in the average Western household, people often dine out. It is uncommon to go to a restaurant and see an African family having dinner unless it is on a special occasion.

Immigrant parents, for the most part, have raised their children on the traditional dishes and less on the mainstream cuisine. Hence, most parents may not know how to make simple Western dishes. However, these parents have children who also love Western cuisines such as pasta, pizzas, chicken wings, apple pie in school, and the larger world around them. A lady explained how she usually gets into an argument with her mom because she doesn't like the dense Ghanaian foods she makes.

> *I don't like Ghanaian food, especially heavy stuff such as fufu and banku, but they force me to eat it, which frustrates me. All she makes is fufu and groundnut soup, waakye, koko, banku, and okra stew. When I eat, I have some unsettledness in my tummy. I try to explain it to my mom so that I could eat something else. She will always tell me that I am lucky even to get food to eat. So, sometimes I eat snacks. I think at least I should have a choice in what to eat.*

> *—Esi, seventeen years old*

Fifteen-year-old Joe explained that he respects the African culture and enjoys most of the Ghanaian dishes his mom makes. He thought they are delicious, but he added:

> *They should take us to restaurants sometimes, or at least, make some non-African food, such as Alfredos, pizzas, or mac, and cheese, instead of always eating at home. It gets one way, you know.*

African immigrant parents grew up in cultures where choices were limited, unlike the Western world where the refrigerator has so much food and drinks. As a child in such cultures, your parents' preferences were your choices. Food was scarce. In these cultures, they prepare food to feed the entire family; a child did not have a decision on what they wanted to eat. Some parents have migrated with the same mindset. Thinking that their children are more fortunate to live in abundance, they interpret any complaints about food choices as ungratefulness.

Often, African parents adopt African dishes instead of Western dishes because they want to transfer their culture to their children. We encourage such parents to maintain their food culture and pass it on to their children. However, we also stress the need to explore other cultures. Since immigrant parents have opted to live in the West with their children, they must be willing to expand their horizons. They should focus on the world of their children and try to adopt certain foods from the mainstream culture, which their children prefer, especially the healthier ones. That way, they can teach their children some African dishes and some dishes from the mainstream culture. Adopting these two food cultures, side by side, is necessary because their children will less likely choose solely African food in their future homes. So, embracing a comprehensive cultural training for their children will set the pace for them to be successful in the future. This approach will also help keep their children from overly depending on fast foods.

A related concept to food choices is chores. In the immigrant home, expectations around chores—the timing and the workload—are often unreasonable. Whether doing homework or engaged in something else, children must drop everything to respond to their parents' calls. In a society where their peers receive rewards for the smallest tasks, children may consider such requests as abusive. In African culture, however, it is common for parents to train their children in home management. Hence, we encourage children to be more receptive to such expectations rather than comparing themselves to their non-African friends. Ultimately, as a young person, you will receive nurturing and experience that will come in handy when you are on your own. Sarah shares that when she went to college, she appreciated all the nagging from her mom to stay in the kitchen and learn how to cook:

> *I can cook by myself and eat whatever I want. The difference now is that I know how to make the African dishes that my mom taught me, and I am free to make any American dish as well. I thought my mom was too extra hard and hated it when I wanted to sleep in on Saturdays, but she would wake me up and force me to do my chores and help her cook. I see the value in all of that now. I feel bad for my friends who can't do the same. Some of my friends rely on their parents to bring them food and even do their laundry for them. I can take care of myself, and that feels good.*

The choice of food and doing chores are issues that parents need to discuss with their children. Since the aim of African parents is, ultimately, to help their children, we encourage that they engage them in more dialogues on such topics. Like the typical Western child, children of immigrant parents want to know why they must do what they do. Therefore, an explanation of why parents ask them to do specific responsibilities will boost their

Like the typical Western child, children of immigrant parents want to know why they must do what they do.

morale and cause them to do these things willingly rather than under coercion. Such dialogues will improve how they receive their parent's cultural values on home management and any advice parents may offer them.

Computers and Social Media

Pew Research found "a major difference in the point of view of younger people and older people today" on eight core values.[24] One of the core values they explored was technology. Almost nine in ten respondents indicated that generations differ in the way they use the internet, computers, and other kinds of technology. Esi describes how her father interacts with technology:

> *Two years ago, I had to set up WhatsApp for my dad, and since I did, he will forward anything that he receives to me and everyone. That can be very annoying, but it is just because he doesn't know how to manage social media. He made me set him up on Facebook as well. I don't even know what he does there. [chuckles]*

> *—Esi, seventeen years old*

Every generation is significantly different from the previous one. The Pew research implies that children of immigrant parents would not behave the same way as their parents on several fronts. Mainstream America with high literacy rates has significant differences in the use of technology for the two generations. In immigrant homes, the difference is more staggering!

The current generation interacts through phones and apps than with people. Besides, they prefer messaging than talking on the phone, and they can spend up to six to seven hours on social media a day. Even phone preference differs between the generations. Grace compares her phone preference with her parents:

> *I prefer an iPhone, and my mom and dad like Android. That is so old school. It took my dad a long time to get me an iPhone.*

But before he did, I had one of my friends give me one to use before I got my own.

—Grace, fifteen years old

Today's youth live their lives on social media and the internet. They are either on their phones, tablets, or computers, doing schoolwork, listening to music, watching movies, playing games, or just attracting the wrong company. The way they use technology is, no doubt, a problem in most homes. Parents often get upset that their children are either doing bad stuff on the internet or failing to do their chores. In instances like this, they may resort to yelling on them to stop using the phone. Yelling, however, often doesn't solve the problem, because the urge to use the phone may be too strong. Some parents decide to take the phones from their children. Even though this approach may work temporarily, youth have several ways to get a new phone. Such denials may compel a lady to easily fall prey to a guy who may be willing to grant her a phone or lure a guy into wrong associations.

Parents can work with their children to set rules on when to use the phone and when to do chores. In doing this, they need to discuss the dangers of the internet and consult with their children so that they will feel part of the decision-making process. Such an inclusive approach will prevent any misunderstandings.

CHAPTER FIVE

I AM HURTING INSIDE, BUT YOU DON'T UNDERSTAND | YOU DON'T APPRECIATE ALL MY SACRIFICES

We have two ears and one mouth so that we can listen twice as much as we speak.—Epictetus

"Efani, come downstairs and sit with the family. Why is everyone together watching TV and you are up in your room? What are you doing there?"

Mrs. Amoah stands at the edge of the stairs and calls her daughter, Efani, who is upstairs in her room.

Efani doesn't bother to come out of her room. So she yells out to her mother. *"I did all you asked me to do and just wanted some time alone to relax. I don't want to watch TV and . . ."*

"You don't want to watch what? This is not the first time. Recently, you are behaving like you have an issue with all of us."

89

Mrs. Amoah angrily interrupts as she walks upstairs to Efani's room. She enters Efani's room and continues her rambling.

"Didn't you see there's no food in the fridge? Why didn't you think of cooking for your brother and sisters before I got home?"

Efani sits on her bed, looking away. *"I don't know. I am so frustrated."*

"What did you say?" Mrs. Amoah inquired.

"Never mind." Efani sharply interjects.

"Ahhh! What do you mean, never mind, Efani?"

[Efani silently to herself]

"What do you expect? I feel like I am living with some evil stepparents. Instead of trying to understand what's wrong, you assume I have a problem with you."

"Ma, you always complain about everything I do, and it's tiring. I am not hungry, and if they are hungry, they are old enough to make something for themselves. I am tired of living in this house."

"Tired of what?" Mrs. Amoah is losing her temper. *"You don't pay bills, you don't work, so what are you tired from doing? We do everything for you, and instead of being grateful, this is what we get, huh. Don't make me angry and call your father."*

[Efani silently to herself] *"Call him, what's new, it's the same thing every day, and I can't stand you. Leave me alone, dang. Do you know what my mind is doing to me? I can't control my mind or anything in my life, and instead of being my safe zone, you are just making everything worse."*

Efani lifts her eyes and now talks directly to her mother. She chokes on her tears.

"Ma, I am not doing anything now because I haven't found a job yet, and it's not like I am not trying. You treat me like a maid and not a daughter, I don't ever get a thank you, but for all I do, it's always criticisms. You always have something negative to say about everything. Gosh! What do you want from me?"

"What? Who do you think you are talking to? What is wrong with you? You have no respect at all, do you? You think just because we are in America, you can talk to me however you want? Why have you become like this? You are not the daughter I raised."

"Please, how did I talk to you? Why can't you listen to me? You see, I am not the same, but has it ever occurred to you to ask me what's wrong? Instead, you make it all about you? Forget you. I am out of here; you are not the mother who raised me either! Can you please leave me alone."

[Mrs. Amoah leaves her room and joins the family downstairs.]

[Silently to herself with tears in her eyes] "God, what have I done so wrong to deserve all this? This life isn't worth living.

I can't take it anymore. I can't get my life together and feel like such a failure. I have no one who understands me, not even my mother; why me, God, why?"

Stressed Parents

The exchange between twenty-five-year-old Efani and her mom is common in most immigrant homes where a lot of cultural tension exists. In these homes, the most straightforward issues look complicated. A simple answer or gesture, which could mean nothing more than "It is okay" in the mainstream culture may sound disrespectful to the African immigrant parent. Such misunderstandings compel children to keep things to themselves. Instead of trying to understand why their children act this way, often, immigrant parents assume there is something wrong with them. Such disagreements are due to the different perceptions of their respective worlds and struggles.

In the Western world, immigrant parents must manage their children in an environment with values that are different from what they know. Meanwhile, their children adopt a new culture. The only way to find the right balance is when parents play a mediating role for their children in this cultural tension, guiding them on what to adopt and what to leave out. However, often, African parents don't know the host culture that well to play that role effectively. Hence, they assume the culture is all bad and try to push the African culture on their children. But such an approach results in increased conflict and unnecessary frustration. In Efani's case, her mother didn't understand why she was behaving that way. Because the African culture focuses on advising, more so than dialoguing, Efani's mom thought she had encouraged her enough, but since Efani is disrespectful, she doesn't want to listen. On the other hand, Efani is struggling with deep emotional issues that require that her mom sit down and talk to her to understand her better. This dialogue never happens—meanwhile, Efani's mother keeps criticizing her. In the end, mom stresses, and Efani is fed-up.

As our daughter neared her teen years, she started using the phrase "Never mind." Initially, I (Cynthia) thought she was snobbish. I would often chastise her and instruct her not to use that phrase again. I was always upset anytime she used that phrase. However, because it was a standard language at school, she could hardly go a day without using it. So, she would mistakenly use it and apologize. Anytime I chastised her, I realized she was confused. So, I decided to have a chat with her on that topic. When I bothered to ask about what she meant whenever she uses "never mind," I uncovered the unknown. Her "never mind" simply means "I don't want to talk about it," "Don't bother about it," or "I feel shy or uncomfortable discussing it" and not "Leave me alone" or "Don't meddle in my business." Reflecting on it, I realized my disapproval of that phrase was a bit of a stretch. I did not have any proof that it was inappropriate. I was stressing myself out and confusing the poor girl. I realized then that at her age, there are some things she was keeping to herself, and I was stopping her short of telling me because I wasn't even allowing her to express her initial thoughts. I observed that sometimes her "Never mind" was testing my reaction to some conversation she wanted to bring up.

On one occasion, after I picked her up from her middle school, we stopped by the elementary school to pick up her younger siblings. We waited in the car at the parking lot for the closing bell to ring. In our usual mother-daughter chats, she raised a sensitive boy-girl conversation that was going on among some kids in her class. At that point, I wanted to probe further, and as I expected, she used her usual phrase, "Never mind." Then, instead of shutting her up,

I told her I was interested in knowing what she wanted to say. She wasn't expecting this response from me, so she looked at me from the corner of her eyes. I pretended as if I didn't see that and asked, "That is interesting; what were they saying?" That offered us a rare opportunity to discuss a critical issue circulating among her peers.

Most immigrant parents struggle to spend time with their children. Part of the reason is, unlike the average Western parent most immigrants deal with long working hours and menial jobs. Most of them lack the necessary educational level to secure a decent job, and some also have to deal with documentation issues. The more fortunate ones who have the means to go back to school end up juggling school and work. Regardless of the situation they find themselves in, combining school, multiple or extended shifts, and the

Immigrant parents must understand that just as adjusting in a different environment can be challenging for them, so it is for their children.

role of parenting puts a lot of stress on such parents. The work schedules of most immigrant parents make it difficult for them to spend time with their children, even if they want to. Sixteen-year-old Fausty, who participated in the focus group, expresses her frustrations about her parents' work schedules:

> *I barely see my parents. They both work two jobs, so they are always stressed out. Instead of helping us with stuff, they want to go to sleep whenever they get a little time. So, we are living with them, but we feel distant. When I complain, they get mad and tell me they need to go to work so they can put food on the table. I don't think they know me.*

Despite the several stresses that immigrant parents deal with, their children often do not totally appreciate their situation. These children expect that, regardless of their busy schedules, parents should be there for their emotional and other needs. Such expectations put undue pressure on immigrant parents and cause a lot of pain for the child who wants more than what their parents can provide.

The fact that immigrant parents are not readily available also limits their ability to support their children with schoolwork and decisions concerning education. This situation sometimes undermines parental authority. A thirteen-year-old describes her difficulties in school:

> *I feel so alone sometimes; I wish my parents were educated like my friends' parents. I sometimes cry because no one is there to help me with my homework. So, yes, I'm not quite in the same position as them [my friends]. My mom has no idea about my homework. She can't help me, and yet, she will be yelling at me to do my homework and all that. How do I do it if I don't get it? Sometimes we are assigned projects, which an adult could have assisted you in getting your materials and all that, but like, I must do all these myself. Sometimes, I ask why I have to do all this by myself. I have lost motivation for school. I do whatever I can, and I don't care much about my grades, because I don't think anyone cares anyway, so what's the big deal?*
>
> *Gladys, thirteen years old*

Immigrant parents must understand that just as adjusting in a different environment can be challenging for them, so it is for their children. However, the type of difficulties their children face may be different because their experiences are not the same. Knowing this would enable them to empathize with their children's issues rather than sweeping their problems under the carpet, thinking that life is easy for them just because they were born in the Western world.

Youth and Stress

Everyone, regardless of age, race, or status, experiences stress. But for youth, this could even be more intense. The youthful stage is when a lot of developmental changes occur. At that stage, unrealistic academic, social, or family expectations may create a strong sense of pressure. The inability to meet these expectations could lead to feelings of failure or even rejection. Young people need to deal with several familial issues at home, and they must also confront expectations and problems that may arise in the school environment. Since they are often not mentally developed to effectively handle some of these issues, such pressures cause a lot of stress.

Stress in the young person's life may be worsened by the conflicting messages that they receive from parents, on the one hand, and friends and society at large, on the other end of the spectrum. Today's youth see more of what life has to offer—both good and bad—on television, at school, in magazines, and on social media. The effect of this overload of information can be very harsh. It is at this stage in life that youth need adult guidance to navigate through life's challenges and to maneuver through all their emotional and physical changes. In the absence of such a support system, they can be stressed, unhappy, emotionally unstable, or even depressed. This condition can potentially affect them in so many ways if the necessary support is not available.

It is not surprising that incidents of depression are increasing at an alarming rate among youth. Research indicates that one in five teens suffers from clinical depression. Depression is a serious problem that calls for prompt and appropriate treatment. It can take several forms, including bipolar disorder, major depressive disorder, persistent depressive disorder, and psychotic depression. All types of depression disrupt the normal functioning of an individual and put them at risk. Depression is sometimes challenging to detect in young people because of their constant mood swings. Also, adolescents do not always understand or express their feelings very well, and so sometimes they are not even aware of the symptoms of depression. Parents and young people must be conversant with the symptoms of depression to enable them to act accordingly when the need arises. The signs of depression include any of these, particularly when they last for more than two weeks:

- *Sadness and hopelessness*
- *Feelings of being unable to satisfy ideals*
- *Poor self-esteem or guilt*
- *Indecision, lack of concentration, or forgetfulness*
- *Lack of enthusiasm, energy, or motivation*
- *Restlessness and agitation*
- *Withdrawal from friends and activities*
- *Changes in eating or sleeping patterns*
- *Anger and rage*
- *Poor performance in school*
- *Substance abuse*
- *Self-cutting*
- *Suicidal thoughts or actions*

Some young people often experiment with drugs or alcohol to avoid feelings of depression. Others may cut themselves, either to numb the pain or to seek attention. Some also express their depression through hostile, aggressive, and risk-taking behavior. But such actions only lead to new problems. Depressive tendencies could also lead to destroyed relationships with friends, family, school officials, or issues with law enforcement agencies. The sad truth, however, is that as a parent, you cannot easily detect such dysfunctions in your child. Most families who experience suicidal death did not know that their child had such tendencies. So, even though risk factors associated with depression may seem glaring, it would take a parent who closely watches and monitors a child to detect these behaviors. That will only be possible if the parent has a close relationship with that child.

A healthy parent-child relationship indeed remains a powerful remedy to some of these emotional problems facing young people. As a parent, you must strive to understand their world, struggles, and fears. You must nurture a loving relationship in your home rather than throwing directives and expectations at them—this can prevent a potential fatality in your own home.

A Different Kind of Stress

Immigrant families undergo adjustments in Western culture, but for their children, it is a double adjustment: *cultural* and *developmental*. In the immigrant home, children often deal with issues that would have been handled by an adult in an average Western family. In homes where parents have limited education, children may assume the roles of mediators or translators in their dealings with social institutions such as schools, hospitals, and social services.[25] This responsibility adds additional pressure to their already full schedules. In homes where parents are more educated, the burden could be less.

In some instances, a young person may feel culturally split, trying to be a dutiful, traditional child at home and an all-American or Western girl/boy at school. It is common to see a sixteen-year-old who is running the household because his or her parents are not fluent in English—that is a lot of stress! From our introduction story to this chapter, it is evident that the immigrant child has additional responsibilities. These children may be less willing to support at home if they feel their parents don't appreciate what they do. Akua from our focus group intimates these feelings:

> *When I get back from school, I am often very exhausted because the day is long. I must then make food for my brothers, clean the dishes, and take out the trash, and I have to do all that before I do my homework, and when my mom comes back from work, I must run several errands for her, and I have to do stuff on the computer for her sometimes. I usually sleep very late, and I am always tired in class. The worse thing is that she doesn't even appreciate all of this.*
>
> —*Akua, sixteen years old*

Many parents expect their children to participate in household chores or take care of their younger siblings. Reluctance to carry out these responsibilities can cause disagreements. Parents should note that as much as they expect their child to help them by following the godly principles in Ephesians 6, their children also need their support and understanding to lighten their tasks. In many immigrant homes, such assistance may not be readily available. For instance, immigrant parents may be less able to academically assist their children outside the family sphere, due to gaps in their understanding of the culture. Outside of the home environment, these children are on their own.

It is the school environment outside the safety of the home where young people face some of the harshest realities of being "different." They deal with name calling, bullying, and racism in different shades and forms. One time, our six your old boy, at that young age, observed and told us, in his innocent voice, that her teacher and classmates always referred to his table (which had two other Caucasian kids) by the names of the other two kids and not his. So, out of curiosity, I (Cynthia) asked him why he thinks they do that. Unexpectedly, he said, *"I think it is because I am the only black kid in there"*. Even at that age, when racism is subtle, immigrant children can feel like the "other(s)". The tendency gets even worse at higher grade levels. All these add up to the stress children deal with, and if they don't have an outlet to pour out such frustrations, the results can be depressive.

A Listening Ear

Generally, African immigrant parents seldom listen to their children. Children of immigrant parents mostly agree that their parents have their own opinions on how they should lead their lives. In the African culture, the parent talks, and the child listens. Growing up in a culture where there is freedom of expression, the youth struggles to take the "do as I say" attitude or succumb to the "listen because I said so" commands.

> *My parents must listen to me when I talk so they won't have many questions like "what did you say?" They should understand my reasons and ideas to help my future and going to college.*

> —*Laura, seventeen years old*

The youth need people who can reason at their level so that they can have open conversations with them about their unique problems. They desire family and friendship support, which are significant social outlets. In their bid to feel belonging and to be understood, they try to find people who are trustworthy and understanding. Their search begins at home, within their close family and friendship circles. Most immigrant families, however, lack this kind of trust. Parents are quick to judge their children as doing something wrong if they realize they are not acting according to what their African culture deems right. Hence, such openness is rare. That may compel some youth to resort to external help, outside of the home. That is, if they find someone who they consider trustworthy. In the worst-case scenario, they hold in their fears and refuse to talk.

> *It's hard for me to open up to my parents about my problems because I know they won't understand what I am going through, so then I tend to keep it in, or I consult with friends even though it would be better for me to talk to an adult.*
>
> *—Ben, fifteen years old*

Some young people go through specific life experiences that are too difficult for their age. These experiences may be traumatizing, but they fear to disclose it to their parents or an adult because of possible victimization. We counseled a twenty-three-year old lady who was dealing with multiple identity crises and suicidal ideations. She narrated to us, after a long period of hesitation, how her cousin abused her for several years. Her parents do not know of this incident because she is afraid to share it with them. The experience has had a devastating effect on her. Her behavior at home has been nothing but troubling. She experiences withdrawal and somatic disorders. The parents, without attempting to have a conversation about her mood swings and actions, just assume she is a stubborn child and call her so many names. Thinking nobody, including her parents, understood her internalizing all the hurt she has had to endure, she felt she was worthless, and life was not worth living.

The way people express their emotions depends on the culture that influences them. Immigrant parents will need to understand that their children express emotions differently from how they (parents) showed their feelings growing up. Parents must understand the implications of their child's actions or reactions in Western culture. The African culture has incredible values that the youth can learn from. However, some values, such as the "culture of silence" can be a killer in youthful Western culture. In that culture, silence could mean numbing your pain and fears. So, as a parent, if you realize that your child is quiet, that could suggest cooperating from your perspective. In Western culture, however, that might signal a deep-seated problem.

The culture of silence in the African immigrant culture has resulted in several incidences of abuse in specific immigrant families. Extended family members or friends may take sexual advantage of young people, knowing very well that they cannot speak up. Due to the likelihood of such unfortunate occurrences, parents must ensure the protection of their children around people, and in some cases, with immediate family. This incidence is more prevalent with children who are sent temporarily to their heritage countries to acquire some disciplinary skills in the African culture. As much as such decisions may be necessary,

The African culture has incredible values that the youth can learn from. However, some values, such as the "culture of silence" can be a killer in youthful Western culture.

parents must ensure that their children's safety is secure because if any abuse occurs, it is most likely the child may never disclose it to you. Still, the negative consequences of the aftermath can never be erased.

Some children are fortunate to have parents with whom they can have open and frank conversations. Others have managed to get mentors who have helped shaped their lives extensively. These have been people who may not necessarily be within the family circle but can play a significant role in shaping the lives of young people. As parents, if you realize the cultural divide is preventing you from forming a strong relationship with your child, it might help to try to acquaint yourself better with the culture. While you are at it, you can assist your child in finding mentors who would provide further guidance and support. Young people should also be proactive in finding mentors who can provide them with the necessary support, besides what their parents can offer, as they adjust in the Western culture with their families.

Undue Comparisons and Self-Worth

In Western culture, we mentioned earlier that children receive a lot of affirmation and praise over the slightest accomplishments. In the immigrant home, such an assertion is rare. Instead, children face verbal abuses at the slightest provocation.

> *My parents always think I do grown-up things. So, when somebody calls me beautiful, they would try to bring me down that I am not. Sometimes the way my mom talks to me, I feel like she thinks I am useless. Everything I do, she complains or insults, like one time I was cooking for her, and I accidentally burned the food and the insult I got. I regretted cooking for her. She always tells me that I am stupid, I have no common sense, and she uses kwasia (fool) a lot. That makes me feel ugly and useless.*
>
> *—Mary, sixteen years old*

I have lost confidence in myself. I am ashamed of who I am and where I come from because of how my parents talk to me.

—*Emmanuel, seventeen years old*

Psychologically, my parents' attitude has kept me in a meta-phorical prison from which I can't escape. If I have an issue I don't like, I have no one to vent or express myself to.

—*Abena, seventeen years old*

The use of abusive language by parents can make youth lose their sense of self-worth. The Bible says: "Do not let any unwholesome talk come out of your mouths, but only what is helpful for building others up according to their needs, that it may benefit those who listen." (Eph. 4:29). Also, in Colossians 3:8: "But now you must rid yourselves of all things as these: anger, wrath, malice, slander, and filthy language from your lips." The way you speak to your child demonstrates what overflows from your heart. As a parent who is a Christian, your heart should overflow with the love of God, which does not discourage or demean. You are to speak positive words to your children. Children feel slandered when they are accused of wrongdoing when, in fact, they are innocent. Examples of abusive language include phrases such as "you are good for nothing," "you will amount to nothing," or "fool." Besides, some expressions may be less harmful in Africa, but in the Western world, they could have severe emotional implications. For instance, in Western culture, if you refer to your child as "fat," it can be demeaning and destructive. We heard a story of how a visiting

> *The words that you speak to your children carry power.*

pastor from Africa visited a church in the United States. This pastor was praying for a young lady who was a bit heavy. This pastor yelled, "You have eaten so much chicken in America, and see how fat you have become." This young girl felt so embarrassed. Her self-esteem was crushed.

Already, youth struggle to find an identity in a racially charged environment. So, when names such as "a fool," "you are good for nothing," and "you are slow" are used on them, they may start acting out those personalities. The words that you speak to your children carry power. By those words, you are shaping their character and influencing their future. Job 22:28 (KJV) says that "Thou shalt decree a thing and it shall be established unto thee….." Immigrant parents often use words loosely on their children and just shrug off the seriousness of their actions by saying, "Oh, I was just joking; they are kids." Such parents must know that what your children hear you say about them continually is what they become.

In some African immigrant homes, parents often compare their children to them growing up and make their children feel they are not as good as them. Besides, some parents compare their children's character and academic abilities to their peers or siblings. In a society where people feel less than what they are worth, such comparisons could be damaging. Some of the young people in our focus group expressed the following concerns:

> *When I don't do well in class, and my parents see my grades, then they start comparing my grades to my sisters, and then they get mad about it. I think we don't have the same abilities. My sisters are different from me. I am good at mathematics, and my sister is good at English. Mary, my other sister, is an all-rounder. I am just good at mathematics and can get all As in it, but my parents don't get that. It is not that I want to go and do law or something. They get on my nerves. I don't even care anymore.*

—Ebenezer, seventeen years old

My mom must control the yelling. She should stop comparing me and encourage me more. She should just stop forcing her way into my way; it is not helping.

—Barbara, eighteen years old

Parents should try to understand our lives better. They shouldn't compare our lives to when they were in Ghana.

—Kakra, sixteen years old

Parents must understand the strengths and giftings of their children; children have different abilities. You should realize that not everyone will become a medical doctor, an engineer, or a nurse. You can use the knowledge of your children's skills to positively urge them to do better in other areas of their lives. For instance, some young people may be good at sports. Such people should not be attacked negatively in areas where they are struggling. Instead, parents can encourage and direct them to maximize their potential in not only sports but other important aspects of their lives.

I don't feel good at all when I don't get an "A." And I can't play a sport because my parents don't attend my games. All they care about is my grades, but I feel I am a gifted soccer player. They don't see that.

—Elijah, sixteen years old

Some youth are exceptionally talented in sports and the arts, and if they are allowed and supported to pursue their passion alongside their academics, it will go a long way to improve their self-esteem and drive. The support would mean that parents attempt to attend their sporting and other extra-curricular events as much as they can. Besides, they should verbally express their support for them in other ways. Such support will ensure that they feel good about themselves and feel accepted. We believe children must be pushed to the extent to which parents believe is their potential. But, since the goal of such a push is to enhance their overall outcomes, using healthy approaches would produce more positive results.

I Don't Want to be Different

Just like every human needs food and shelter, a sense of belonging is a human need. *Belonging* means acceptance as a member or part of a group. Fitting in or gaining peer acceptance for many adolescents is more important than academic goals because it adds value to life and increases their ability to cope. When you see your connection to others, you know that all people struggle and have difficult times; you realize you are not alone. In other instances, having a sense of belonging makes you feel accepted and not different from others.

You should realize that not everyone will become a medical doctor, an engineer, or a nurse.

Some youth find belonging in a church, some with friends, some with family, and others on social media. While some see themselves as connected only to one or two people, others believe and feel a connection to all people the world over. Young people may have a circle of physical friends and a bunch of virtual friends. Within these social networks exist norms and values. These values may include how to dress, types of fashion, brand names to adopt, relationships, and social life such as drinking and partying, and so on. The high-tech culture has facilitated this trend, and in these fast and furious days of digital overload, parents often worry about their children's interactions with one another on social media and within their world. Parents who perceive the host culture as too lax on several values often attempt to protect or restrain their children from any significant cultural influences of this sort. Such parents often refuse sleepovers, play dates, and parties, especially those that go into the night. They are often more comfortable if their children hang out with other immigrant families or families they know.

> *I can sleep over Ghanaian homes but never a friend from school. I have a lot of Caucasian friends, and they hang out in their homes, which is kind of fun, but I always feel left out. It's hard for me to keep explaining why my parents wouldn't like me to sleepover at least sometimes. One time, I am like, "My dad was at work, so I needed to take care of my sister", when my friends requested a sleepover. The next time, I wasn't sure what reason to give. It makes me feel dumb and left out when I am with my friends, and that stresses me out . . . like so much. I feel weird.*
>
> —*Kobby, sixteen years old*

The youth from immigrant homes need to navigate and negotiate between their heritage culture and the host culture while finding acceptance and belonging within their unique subculture. When parents deal with a child who is struggling for recognition through such social cliques, they should appreciate these struggles and explain the rationale behind any restrictions. For instance, if you wouldn't agree to a sleepover, it will help if you can explain why instead of just saying no. You can then talk to the child to figure out a way to cope.

When our first child was nine, she started requesting sleepovers at her friends' homes [non-Africans]. We usually wouldn't allow a sleep-over at any person's home unless the person is a family member. We had to explain to her that we are interested in her having fun with her friends. However, since we were not familiar with who lived in the house and who may have contacts with the girls in our absence, we were not comfortable. We explained further that her security was our utmost priority. So, we made a deal. For any girls' sleepover, we would turn it into a night play date for her, and we would pick her up at 9:00 p.m., while the other girls continued through the night. She completely understood our rationale, and her friends respected her decision. She accepted it and articulated it in a way that made sense to her friends. She is now a teenager, and we still have a deal.

Most immigrant families have similar cultural values. Nonetheless, what is considered right or wrong, appropriate or inappropriate, varies from family to family. Parents should find reasonable ways to negotiate with their children on such issues so they don't shut these children up and cause them unnecessary emotional pain.

One controversial issue within immigrant families relates to appearance. Fashion is a hot topic among youth. It gives them a sense of belonging to specific groups. Growing up in Africa, it was common for immigrant parents to wear the same pair of shoes for a couple of years. Their children, however, who are born or raised in the West live in a materialistic culture. A new iPhone or Android phone is released every six months. Fashion magazines show different trends every season. As a young person, failure to adopt the trends or styles makes them feel left out. Even though adapting to the trends is a big deal for the average youth, for the parent, such issues may be irrelevant. Ironically, the feeling that you do not belong can lead to a sense of rejection, depression, and even suicidal tendencies among young people. Erica, a fifteen-year-old girl, narrates her ordeal with not having trendy items at school:

> *My parents sometimes don't feel the need to buy me new things because they say I have enough or "you already have one." But the thing is, everyone uses a new item and, it is the one trending, and if you don't have one, it makes you look cheap, you know . . . and different; it's, like, why? You can't get these cool shoes, or sneakers, or even phone? Sometimes, I don't feel like going to school because I know people will make fun of me.*
>
> —*Erica, fifteen years old*

Erica is just one young girl, among the thousands of children in immigrant homes who are dealing with such challenges. Ebenezer expresses similar sentiments about how he feels his parents don't understand what he goes through as a young person dealing with trends and a sense of belonging:

> *Parents don't understand how kids are in today's society, for example, with regards to clothing, school, gadgets, etc. My mom won't just understand me. Sometimes, I am like, "I want an iPhone." Everyone uses an iPhone at school, and if you have an Android, they make fun of you." I am always, like, "Can you just get your Android and get me my iPhone?" She gets upset when I say this, and she thinks I am rude, but it's not that; I just feel like a jerk, and I always must hide my Android phone. She just doesn't get it that it is the trend now, and it's our time. [laughs]*
>
> —*Ebenezer, sixteen years old*

Here, we are not condoning the unlimited access to material things. We advise against giving a child everything they want. However, parents should explain to their children for them to understand why they can't have what they are asking for, rather than ignoring them. In the school setting, certain things are a given. For instance, a pair of sneakers, a shirt brand, or a phone type may

After all, even as adults, we patronize laces, clothes, bags, and shoes that are in vogue, so why can't we at least do the same for our children?

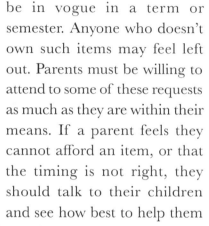

be in vogue in a term or semester. Anyone who doesn't own such items may feel left out. Parents must be willing to attend to some of these requests as much as they are within their means. If a parent feels they cannot afford an item, or that the timing is not right, they should talk to their children and see how best to help them deal with the pressure to own that item. After all, even as adults, we patronize laces, clothes, bags, and shoes that are in vogue, so why can't we at least do the same for our children? They are more vulnerable and susceptible to the harsh culture of comparison? If adults struggle with such appearance-related issues, how much more a young person who is not strong enough to deal with some of these emotional issues.

Just as young people desire some personal items, they also want some time and space with their friends.

They just don't understand my life. They always ask, "Why are you on your phone?" like, all the time. Taking away my phone doesn't even help the problem. They just don't understand that people judge when you are not on social media, and when you don't watch the latest shows, you seem like an outcast. You feel left out when they talk about the shows and all that, and you don't have a clue about what is happening on the screens.

—Eric, fifteen years old

Who hasn't seen a teenager deeply absorbed with a smartphone or breaking off a face-to-face conversation to take a picture for their friends on Snapchat? Seeing your children with their heads down on the screens of their phones can feel annoying. Today's adolescents live much of their lives on social media and the internet; that is where they do their homework, find solutions to their problems, meet new friends, catch up on shows, and so on. Hence, they get frustrated when parents limit their cell phone usage or complain about why they are always on the phone rather than talking to them.

Inasmuch as social media is trendy, uncontrolled usage can be damaging. Some youth have poor grades in school due to social media addiction; others have hooked into wrong associations. In some cases, lives may be at stake. Two years ago, a middle-aged lady who called us for counseling narrated how her sixteen-year-old daughter had hooked up with a sixty-year-old man in California. According to her, her daughter and this man were engaged in long-distance sexual relations via social media. The man was at that point of planning for the sixteen-year-old daughter to join him in California for sexual pleasure. It took the divine intervention of God to save this poor girl. But the question is, how many young people fall victim to such perverts due to excessive and uncontrolled social media usage?

Considering the dangers of the social media world, we suggest to the youth that they should not take their parents' advice on social media usage as cynical. Of course, parents and children should collaboratively set boundaries with the prevailing culture in mind. Parents should aim to strike a balance between giving them some space and providing supervision and guidance. Likewise, young people should also know that uncontrolled usage of the phone and social media has several implications on their education, emotions, health, and their overall future. Even though you might think your parents are not tech savvy, they know more about the dangers of the lack of self-control than you do. Hence, heeding their advice on limited usage will keep you out of a lot of trouble.

Handling Stressed Youth in the Immigrant Home

In immigrant homes, trust is the key. It creates a balance between respecting your child's privacy and probing into his or her life. In the absence of trust, youth tend to stay away and keep things to themselves. Keeping to themselves, however, does not mean they are emotionally stable; what it means is "I am trying to figure things out in my world." One mother, Florence, we spoke to, and later handled the rift between her and her teenage daughter, narrated how she hardly went to her daughters' room because anytime she did, the daughter got upset. She didn't know what was in that room and what went on there. As we continued the conversations, we advised her to try and spend time with her daughter and to find a way to also go into her "personal space" to make sure she was okay. The parent was shocked to see that somewhere in the daughter's closet, she had written these words to express her hidden emotions:

> *I wish my mom were dead [with the death emoji], I hate her so much. I know she hates me too; that is why she doesn't care about me. I don't feel like I have a mom. I just feel like I live with a tigress. . . . [smh]. . . . die!!! And I wish I wasn't born in the first place. I shouldn't live [the crying emoji]!*

113

This find made the mom furious, and she confronted her daughter when she returned from school:

> *Florence (mother): So you want to see me dead. Aahhhh! Come and kill me! After everything I have done for you, you want me dead. After all the sacrifices to put food on the table for you, you want me dead. Hmm, I don't even know what to tell you anymore. I am so tired of you. I can't deal with you either! If you don't need me, your sisters and brother need me. I will not die today or tomorrow. I will live to take care of my other children who care about me.*

At that instant, the daughter who said nothing rushed to her "safe zone," her bedroom. She sobbed all evening and wouldn't come out of her room.

When we got the chance to sit down with the mom, we explained to her that she seemed to be focusing on herself alone, without considering her daughter's feelings. We advised that it was necessary for her to at least listen to her daughter on why she felt the way she did. The discussion made this mom see things differently. All along, she perceived her daughter as an awkward teenager, and she decided to ignore her. She now found out that she needed to reconsider how she treats her rather than focusing on just how the daughter responds to her.

The mom went ahead and had a conversation with her daughter. She discovered

A young person's expression of indifference, anger, moodiness, withdrawal from family and friends, and poor self-esteem may be the evidence of a deep-seated problem, which could culminate in suicidal tendencies.

that her undue restrictions, such as not allowing playdates and sleepovers, and not buying certain things that she needed for her, made her daughter feel left out. This lady did not have a good relationship with her parents, and she also felt her mother denied her access to the friends that made her happy. She observed that her peers enjoy more privileges than her, so she assumed her mother didn't want her to be happy. She completely misunderstood her mother's good intentions for setting those restrictions because her mother did not clearly communicate her intentions to her; she was always yelling. After our encounter with this family, the mother decided to discuss and negotiate these privileges with her daughter. She also made it a point to spend more time with her.

The youth growing up in Western culture may have different interpretations of specific actions than their immigrant parents. Therefore, as a parent, it is necessary to dialogue more with them on such matters. In the case of Florence's family, her daughter got a timely intervention, which prevented potential depression. If the issue lingered, it could have developed into suicidal tendencies because the writings in the closet pointed to death. Such discoveries should not be trivialized because they suggest deep emotional issues your child may be dealing with. In one instance, a gentleman we counseled had given up on his family and life in general and decided to end it all. He was sexually abused and felt no one understood him. At the point of attempting to kill himself, he withdrew from school, and was in his room contemplating this for days. We encountered him at the right time, and that stopped any move in the wrong direction.

A young person's expression of indifference, anger, moodiness, withdrawal from family and friends, and poor self-esteem may be the evidence of a deep-seated problem, which could culminate in suicidal tendencies. If you observe any of these signs in your child, it is necessary to probe carefully and lovingly to help them rather than push them away. Studies have shown that four out of five people who attempt suicide have given clear warnings. As a parent, it is necessary to pay attention to these warning signs in your child as an indication of an emotional problem that needs your attention:

- *Suicide threats, direct and indirect*

- *Obsession with death*

- *Poems, essays, and drawings that refer to death*

- *Giving away belongings*

- *A dramatic change in personality or appearance*

- *Irrational, bizarre behavior*

- *An overwhelming sense of guilt, shame, or rejection*

- *Changed eating or sleeping patterns*

- *Severe drop in school performance*

A significant fallout from these emotional issues that young people deal with is the need for immigrant parents to realize that the mental and emotional health of their children is as important as their physical health. Historically, mental health didn't receive a lot of attention on the health and development policy agenda in Africa due to seemingly more pressing issues such as poverty and diseases. Besides, people trivialize the extent of mental health problems and assume it is untreatable.

Mental health is one area where African immigrant parents can compromise specific cultural values to save their children.

Research indicates that African Americans and Africans believe that mild depression or anxiety would be considered "crazy" in their social circles. Furthermore, many believe that discussions about mental illness would not be appropriate even among family circles. Sadly, African immigrant families have imported the same perception of mental health into the Western environments within which they live. Due to this perception, most families fail to seek help for themselves or their children should they face mental health challenges.

Ironically, mental health issues and emotional instability are prevalent among youth. One in five teens has a psychological problem, such as depression, anxiety, attention deficit disorder, substance use, and panic disorders. The immigrant child is part of this story; their case may even be worse, considering the multicultural and multigenerational issues they face. Fortunately, in mainstream Western culture, people can talk about mental health issues. Therefore, we encourage African parents living in the West to take advantage of this openness and engage their children in such matters. We understand that they would like to preserve some of their cultural values. However, sometimes doing so could adversely affect the lives of their children. Mental health is one area where African immigrant parents can compromise specific cultural values to save their children.

Communication and open talk are essential building blocks to nurture discussions on seemingly difficult topics like mental health. We advocate a relationship-based style of parenting in immigrant homes so children can be comfortable sharing their problems with family members, without any shame. We further suggest that besides any support at home, such as spiritual intervention, in some instances, families may need external emotional assistance. If the need arises, they must not feel shy to ask for such help, either through the church or professional counseling, therapy or treatment.

CHAPTER SIX

LIFE IS NOT ALL
ABOUT CHURCH |
YOU WILL GO TO CHURCH!

The stone was rolled away from the door, not to permit Christ to come in, but to enable the disciples to go in.—Peter Marshall

Most churches in our world today cater to the spiritual and emotional needs of the older generation, but not so much to the younger generation. Even though some churches have youth ministries, there is usually a bias towards the adult population. Or, better put, most of these churches are not able to meet the unique spiritual and emotional needs of the younger generation. It is not surprising that churches are losing people from this age category.

The youth's departure from the mainstream church is not different in immigrant churches. The reason for the current trend is that young people have embraced several worldviews regarding religion and doctrines, which have left them confused.[26] Their exposure to such worldviews has resulted in several unanswered questions. They know they cannot ask their questions in the church because people will see them as "departing from the faith." They, therefore, sit in pews, quiet and confused. Others just leave. What complicates the situation for immigrant families is that most youth from these homes think their parents hardly engage them in conversations that are relevant to their age and culture at home, besides issues about church and education. So, the average child growing up in an immigrant home neither gets answers to his or her questions at church nor at home.

In a recent interaction with nineteen-year old Ray, he expressed how he wished his parents related to him in his passion for sports and his unique challenges as a young black man growing up in America. Ray yearns for frank talk about sex, transition into adulthood, basketball, and issues that his parents consider too sacred or trivial. His church, on the other hand, hardly engages in such youth-related topics. Like the average youth, the lack of relevance on such issues forces Ray to look outside the walls of his home and church for help.

Most African immigrants believe that their lives, well-being, and progress depend on the sovereign God. For them, the only way they and their children can make it in a foreign land is to put God first. In the immigrant Christian home, parents train their children to appreciate that church is the ultimate solution to all of life's challenges. They teach them from their early days in Sunday school that if you "read your Bible and pray every day," you will grow. Several young people, therefore, follow their parents to church out of compulsion.

Meanwhile, in most churches, the worship style, the medium of communication, and the content of sermons may carry little relevance to the younger generation. As these young people sit in their "parents' traditional churches," they "tune-out" and "tune in" to their favorite social media pastors, such as Mike Todd, Steven Furtick, or Sarah Jakes. For these youth, even mainstream televangelists like Bishop J. D. Jakes and Joyce Meyers are outdated. They begin to "have a church within a church." Others simply play games on their phones. When the adults confront them about not paying attention, they just sneak outside of the service or go to a bathroom to avoid further confrontations.

It is common to enter a church today and find many of the teenagers sitting at the back. They usually have their iPhones in their hands, scrolling through Instagram, YouTube, or another social media page, while the pastor is ministering the Word of God. If they cannot find meaning in the style and message of the worship service, they tune off and tune out.

> *For the younger generation, rules without relationships don't mean much to them.*

Today's youth will not productively engage in the church if they don't feel engaged. They don't want to feel compelled to go to church; they want to go because it is engaging and fulfilling. For the younger generation, rules without relationships don't mean much to them.

With the massive emphasis on belonging to a church, the young people are beginning to ask: "Is life all about the church? What's in church for me?" Their willingness to stay in the church depends on the answers they get for these questions.

Can the Church Provide Answers?

Most immigrant families are religious. In contrast, many young people feel the church has offered them half-baked answers to their thorny and honest questions[27]. Some have therefore turned their backs to the church and rejected the talking heads and condemnatory outlook that they see among the older generation. They wonder: "At home, my parents don't understand me, and at church, they consider me disrespectful or doing the bad stuff if I probe into issues. So, where do I go?"

Several youth are contending for their identity and faith. Specifically, youth are always seeking acceptance. They desire a place where they will discover themselves, deepen their faith, and fulfill their destinies. The fact that they have African ancestry but live on Western soil leaves them wondering where they truly belong. To belong here and there, these young people negotiate between both cultures and may create a unique spiritual culture of their own. In our ministry to campuses, we realize that the African students on the universities have their organizations and way of doing things. They feel belonging among peers who share a similar background as them. When you ask about their background, they are quick to say they are from an African country. Nonetheless, they seek one thing: to find God through authentic Christian fellowship.

The churches that seek to engage these young people must, therefore, create an accepting, forward-looking, welcoming, and authentic environment for them. These churches may not necessarily have answers to many of their questions. If they demonstrate genuine love and authenticity and a willingness to adjust to suit the needs of the current generation, it can make a big difference. These realities should also prompt immigrant parents and church leaders to realize that forcing youth to go to church is not the path to real transformation. Martin Luther and his colleagues could not enforce any real reformation without abandoning the status quo.[28] Similarly, young people desire a change, but that can only be possible if parents and church leaders provide the right environment for that change.

What we would like to stress here is that unlike how most people see youth, they love the church, and they love God. What they don't appreciate is coming to church for the sake of coming and worshipping a God they can't relate to. They are frustrated with the shallow expressions of religion. Some young people have said, "I want to be part of a Christian community or a church that is more than a performance three days a week." They want a church that is full of life and the Holy Spirit. They want a church that expresses authentic faith in and out of its four walls. They want a church that has a plan to transform cultures and societies.

To meet the spiritual needs of this current generation, churches must make some adjustments in their worship styles and context.

The quest for cultural relevance in our churches is not a call to bend biblical standards to fit into today's culture. Instead, it is a call to demonstrate Christian virtues in a culturally appropriate way.

Building a relevant church for youth also requires that the church is willing to meet their deep-seated needs. Many will respond to an authentic worship experience regardless of the cultural differences if you carry a solution to their heartfelt needs and cries.

The quest for cultural relevance in our churches is not a call to bend biblical standards to fit into today's culture. Instead, it is a call to demonstrate Christian virtues in a culturally appropriate way. It is a desire to belong, which is in the heart of every young person. The church should be the conduit through which every longing heart will be satisfied. This sense of belonging is what today's generation is crying for—to belong to a family of God, a community of caring people. In the absence of such an environment, young people will find other means to satisfy their deep spiritual longing. They may leave the church. Often, however, outside of Christ, there is nothing that can fulfill their weary souls (Ps. 107:9).

Why They Leave the Church

Many young people in the Western world have given several reasons why they leave their churches. Some cite a lack of involvement. In some instances, when the leadership fails to integrate the younger generation into church activities and administration, they become indifferent. Some older people may want to hold on to every position of influence until their last breath. When this happens, the emerging generation may remain untrained and ill-equipped to take on the leadership mantle. A Nigerian pastor friend narrated that in his church, this lady in her sixties who could barely walk would force herself to administer her duties. Let's be clear here. We are not saying all those in their sixties should step back and allow those in their twenties and thirties to take over. No! There are people in their sixties who are strong enough to still do the work. What we suggest is that for the younger generation to belong and have a sense of purpose in the church, the older generation must work side by side with them, without feeling threatened.

Paul worked side-by-side with Timothy, Elijah worked side by side with Elisha, and Moses worked side by side with Joshua. The coworking relationship between these duos resulted in smooth transitions in leadership and giftings. In the same way, church leaders must work towards providing clear opportunities for the younger generation to get engaged in the church. The process of passing on the mantle should begin now. Future leaders should start their training and transition into leadership today. Church leadership must be intentional about figuring out the passion and giftings of young people and help to match them up with the right opportunities in the church. In our few years in ministry, we have realized that, when empowered and trusted, young people can do amazing things. These young people are full of energy and are looking for something to do. We need to trust them and make room for them. They may make mistakes, but mistakes are necessary for the growth process.

The older generation should engage the younger generation, and young people must take advantage of such engagements. As a young person, you can create some opportunities for service. Your eyes should not just be set on the pulpit to preach. God's kingdom has more to offer than holding the microphone to sing, lead prayer, or share the Word of God. Among several examples worthy of emulation, we would like to share the story of one young lady at one of the universities, who grew up in the Church of Pentecost. She had some challenges relating to the worship experience at her local church. Then it was time to go to college. She thought to herself, "I would not leave my church. Rather, I would seek help from my **PENSA** (Pentecost students and associates) leaders and start a multicultural **PENSA** ministry on campus. I can be an agent of change." So, with the support of some leaders, she launched out forcefully and started putting some of her friends together to start a student organization, **PENSA**. She got the required number for recognition and successfully navigated the school system for registration.

Today, the organization has grown into a thriving student group. Similar stories abound across the nation, where young people have taken up the challenge to either start student organizations on their campuses or organize the youth in their churches for programs that are relevant to their generation. These campus leaders can potentially transition into the local church and continue their service there. Like these people, you can brighten the corner where you are. We encourage you to get radical for Christ. The potential you carry is enormous, and the mandate is clear. Arise and embrace the countless opportunities to serve in your time.

Agents of Change

The church is in the world; a world with views that are different from biblical standards. As intimated by Jesus in John 17, as Christians, we live in a world with opinions and philosophies that do not align with what defines us. "I have given them your word and the world has hated them, for they are not of the world any more than I am of the world. My prayer is not that you take them out of the world but that you protect them from the evil one. They are not of the world, even as I am not of it." (John 17:14–16). As Christians, the fact that we are in the world does not mean we should bend our biblical stances. For instance, as a young man or woman, your decision to be celibate may be unpopular, but being a child of God, you don't have to go with the beliefs of the world.

Our mandate as followers of Christ is to penetrate secular culture with kingdom culture.

Our mandate as followers of Christ is to penetrate secular culture with kingdom culture. We want to emphasize that the significant weapon for this transformation is the word of God. "Is not my word like fire, says the Lord, and like a hammer that breaks a rock in pieces?" (Jer. 23:29) The word is a hammer that breaks hardened views of the world and gives the believer a penetrating edge. It is sharper than any two-edged sword, capable of bringing redemption to the souls of men. As a high school or college student, you are the "church" on your campus. As a young professional, you are the "church" at your office. You have a mandate to infiltrate your community with kingdom culture. You carry a treasure—the gospel, God's power of salvation for humanity.

We want to throw out a word to all our young readers. Do not consider the church or Christianity as belonging to your parents.

The faith they carry has sustained them over the years. In our world today, most people who have walked away from Christ and the church have come to realize that there is nothing more fulfilling out there in the world. Unlike these people, you must cherish your faith. You should not allow intergenerational conflict at home or some hypocrisy that you have seen in a church to rob you of this precious possession. Despite its weaknesses, the church remains the medium by which God's love and grace flow into many lives, including yours.

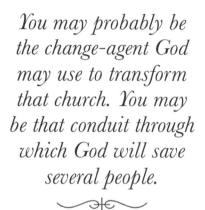

You may probably be the change-agent God may use to transform that church. You may be that conduit through which God will save several people.

You may not be happy with a lot of things in your church. That is normal. After all, the church consists of people from different generations who see and understand things differently. Besides, no church is perfect. Instead of complaining and possibly finding another church, be an agent of change. Don't be too quick to leave. Even if you have to go at all costs, make sure you have explored all options by discussing with your leadership about ways to make the church more relevant and engaging. You may probably be the change-agent God may use to transform that church. You may be that conduit through which God will save several people. In 2004, I (Cynthia) joined a church in the United States. This church was not what I expected. I didn't feel fulfilled; neither was I challenged beyond what I knew. As human as I was, I complained a bit, but I didn't have the option to leave because I loved the church. A year or so after, I decided to do whatever I could to serve. I prayed for direction. With the change of mindset, I started seeing things differently and began to do more to help in the church. I saw the issue as our problem and envisioned myself as part of the solution. I realized the church got better, and I felt fulfilled serving rather than complaining. But what made this possible was that the leadership gave me a platform to serve. Now, this same church has grown into a vibrant and youthful church catering to the spiritual needs of several young people.

Paul admonished Timothy: "Don't let anyone look down on you because you are young, but set an example for the believers in speech, in conduct, in love, in faith, and in purity" (1 Tim. 4:12). In the same way, as a youth, arise, infiltrate the world with the love of God, and bring transformation to our present evil world. This world could be your high school, college campus, or your workplace. We also encourage parents to engage their children in open and frank discussions regarding issues of concern about the church rather than shelving it for another day or just completely ignoring them. This engagement must include regularly scheduled family devotions and meetings. Also, immigrant parents and church leaders should continually engage the youth and create a conducive environment within which they will thrive spiritually and find purpose. That way, when they leave for college, they will not hesitate to return to their home church; they will have found God for themselves rather than worshipping their parents' God.[29]

CHAPTER SEVEN

I CAN'T WAIT TO GO TO COLLEGE | I AM SCARED TO SEE YOU GO

To raise a child who is comfortable enough to leave you means you've done your job. They are not yours to keep, but to teach them to soar on their own.—Author Unknown.

"I can't believe you are leaving soon for college, Oluwa," Mrs. Adeyemi remarks to Oluwa, her daughter, as she sorts out the laundry.

"I am, Mom, and it's more than exciting. I can't wait to leave!" Oluwa answers without looking at her mother. She stirs the *ogbono* soup on the stove.

"Why are you anxious to leave? There's a lot you must learn, and we have not finished training you," her mom eagerly chimes in.

"Mom, I think I have gotten enough of the pressure." Oluwa turns to look at her mother to see her reaction. *"Every day, it's church, church, church. As if life is all about church. Every day, I need to become a nurse, as if I can't*

*make it without that. I can't even have friends so long as I
am under this roof."*

"You deserve a slap." Mrs. Adeyemi walks from the
laundry room to the kitchen where Oluwa is. *"We
do so much for you, and yet you don't see it, and you misin-
terpret our care to be pressure. If you go to church, are you
serving God for me? You break my heart by talking like this."*

"That is exactly the point, mom." Oluwa keeps stirring
the soup. *"If I am not doing it for you, then why don't you
leave me to make my own decisions? Well, I guess I will
continue to be silent until I leave this home. You broke my
heart long ago when I realized you didn't love me, and all
you are thinking is me becoming a nurse so I can come and
take care of you."*

"Ehhhhhhhhhh?" Mrs. Adeyemi couldn't believe her
daughter's reaction.

[Silence]

*"Oluwa, what do you mean? Do you want to be a runaway kid,
like Mr. Bola's boy? Look, in our African culture, as a good
and respectful daughter, you do not even talk about leaving
home until you are ready to marry. And hear what you are
saying today. Nonsense."*

[Oluwa walks out]

"Oluwa! Oluwa! Hmm!"

This conversation is between Oluwa, a seventeen-year-old first-generation American-born lady and her fifty-three-year-old immigrant mother, as she gets ready to leave home for college. Life in the immigrant home may be overwhelmingly dull and daunting for the youth who prefers freedom and exploration instead of a bunch of dos and don'ts. When such young people meet with their fellow high schoolers or college mates, they hear of the freedom these people have in their homes. That amazes them and upsets them at the same time. The question that lingers in their minds is, "Why can't we have just a bit of this freedom?" They see how their peers are free to use social media, have sleepovers, and almost zero house chores. They then assume that their parents are not fair to them.

For youth who face these restrictions, one way to survive is to find avenues for escape. So, when suddenly the reality of going to college sets in, or if they must move out for whatever reason, they see it as an opportune time to just leave, physically, mentally, emotionally, and spiritually. The youth is ecstatic about the reality of leaving home; it is an opportunity to enter the free world to live their lives the way they want to.

We suggest that as much as the youth may be excited to leave, they must pause and rethink their motive for leaving before they do so. It is necessary to make sure the reason for leaving is sound and lines up with God's purpose. Interestingly, some of the young people who have left home to explore a world of freedom and fun found themselves in the wrong company that almost ruined their lives. They realized their parents were a protective shield around them, no matter how culturally irrelevant they thought they were.

Leaving in Love

There is a time for everything (Eccl. 3:1a). A time would come when, as a young person, you will leave for college, be married off, or just leave. Detaching from your parents can be emotional. It is, therefore, necessary to guard those emotions with positive thoughts. In Phil. 4:8, Paul admonishes, "Finally, brothers and sisters, whatever is true, whatever is noble, whatever is right, whatever is pure, whatever is lovely, whatever is admirable—if anything is excellent or praiseworthy—think about such things." Before you leave home, reflect on both the good and challenging times in your relationship with your parents. Such an assessment enables you to step back and ponder over the great times you have had. This period is the time to review memories of exciting family events and celebrations. Simply fill your thoughts with what is lovely, peaceful, and praiseworthy.

Just like one lady who told us, "I can't think of a lot whole of positive memories in my home," you may also feel there is almost nothing to celebrate. If you find yourself in this situation, we suggest that you spend quality time in prayer and ask God to fill your heart with overflowing love. The Holy Spirit can shed the love of God in your heart if you lend yourself to his infilling. Besides, be intentional about letting go of any pain and hurt from the past. Eph. 4:31–32 encourages us to "get rid of all bitterness, rage, and anger, brawling, and slander, along with every form of malice. Be kind and compassionate to one another, forgiving

Before you leave home, reflect on both the good and challenging times in your relationship with your parents.

each other, just as in Christ God forgave you." Know that underneath the bitterness, anger, and disagreement there exists a remnant of love and hope. Dig deep, and you will find something positive to celebrate, for "love covers over a multitude of sins" (1 Pet. 4:8b).

Moments of separation call for not only reflection but also a period of healing. This time is the moment to repair any broken relationships, as much as it is within your means (Rom. 12:18). It will require that you make peace with God, yourself, your parents, and, if necessary, your siblings. If you feel comfortable talking to your parents, this is the time to do so. However, proceed with prayer and patience. In talking to them, just calm yourself and find an excellent way to let them know how you feel. You can also apologize to them if you think you may have wronged them. They may have said certain things that did not make sense to you, but you will realize later down the years that several of the concerns they raised were worth your time and consideration. Reflect on Prov. 13:1: "A wise son heeds his father's instruction, but a mocker does not respond to rebukes." Also, remember that you, too, have not been perfect in many ways, but God forgave you. God is calling on you to do the same to others, including your family members. The love chapter in the Bible, 1 Corinthians 13, presents love as "the excellent way." Let the word of God empower you to choose the path of love, to forgive your parents and others, and love them genuinely before you make any transition; it is the platform for your internal peace, spiritual fervency, and academic success.

As you get ready to transition into adulthood, know that real freedom is when you are emotionally free. There is nothing more burdening to carry in life than bitterness and unforgiveness, mainly if it concerns people close to you. This weight could potentially deprive you of a life of joy, peace, and your overall spiritual strength. Yes, it might be tough sometimes to let go, but God's grace continues to abound for those who are willing to do so. Do not allow the pain of the past to blur your ability to see the bright future that God has in mind for you.

Periods of transition are times to reflect on God's plan for your life, which is a plan of love and fulfillment. As you journey into the next phase of life, developing an attitude of love keeps you under God's protective power when parental presence is not available. If you keep holding on to the grudges and the pains of your relationships, it will be difficult for you to follow God's plan. One practical way to deal with any pain or misunderstandings with parents is to think about their cultural background. They grew up in an entirely different environment. Your grandparents were probably born in the 1940s or earlier, and your parents learned the parenting style from them, which was suitable at the time. In many ways, your parents are products of a culture they did not form; they just received it. It is, therefore, difficult, if not impossible, for them to take on several aspects of the new culture, no matter how much they try. Taking this perspective will offer you a more in-depth insight into their lives and help you overlook some of their shortfalls as a result of your cultural differences.

An immigrant parent-child workshop we held with over 300 immigrant parents and their children opened our eyes to a few things. We realized that most immigrant parents are open to understanding the world of their children. However, they have not been exposed to training and workshops on this topic. If immigrant parents receive training on cultural relevance, they will be more receptive to the culture that is shaping their children. Likewise, if we train the youth to understand that their parents are Africans first before they moved to the West, they can better accommodate their differences. The youth will realize that their parents don't mean to punish them or make them uncomfortable by their actions or inactions. Instead, they act the way they do because that is what they know as godly upbringing. We believe this finding brings some hope for resolving the long-standing cultural battles that exist in immigrant homes. It will also ensure that even if children must leave home, they will do so with their parents' blessings.

The Separation Challenge

For the young person, transition into college can be an exciting and nerve-wracking experience at the same time. However, it is not just them who go through this psychological and emotional challenge; the transition is tough for parents as well. The separation between the parent and the child often leaves a void in the home. One mom commented, "I feel less constrained, I have more time now, but I feel bored sometimes. The loud music is gone, and my car is now always available."

The challenge can be real. Parents may go through a period of loneliness when their child leaves home. The intensity, however, depends on the nature of the relationship that existed between you and your child. After your child leaves for college, you can no longer have direct access to them. That is why it is essential to take advantage of the brief time you spend with them, building a relationship, and transferring your values to them. That way, you will have less worry when they are gone.

Before you leave home, reflect on both the good and challenging times in your relationship with your parents.

At this stage, it is helpful to start relinquishing some parental control. We have discussed the importance of autonomy for youth in this book as an essential aspect of your child's development into adulthood. You must intentionally allow your child to make some decisions on their own. You may or may not be able to keep your firm grip, but so long as they listen to you and discuss things with you, that is just fine. Your child will be more willing to listen and to bring issues to your attention when you have a strong bond with them. So, instead of being unnecessarily strict and pushy, relax, and nurture the relationship while providing the necessary guidance.

It is normal for your child to face specific challenges as they leave home. Parents must be ready to engage them in any discussions that may ensue. You should address issues around finances and roommate arrangements. Also, it might be necessary for you to explore available campus or rental resources and assist your child in accessing these resources, depending on their needs. If you have challenges understanding how to navigate the system, you can identify some godly mentors who will be willing to assist in this critical effort.

When your child leaves home, you can offer them a "parting gift." It can be the Holy Bible, a bag, or something they like. Besides, spend some quality time in providing specific advice one more time. Pray together. Remember, you cannot be with that child everywhere they go, but God can. He is omnipresent. Ask God to protect and guide your child, and ask for wisdom and understanding.

When your child leaves, decide to stay in touch with them through phone and video calls and visit when possible. All these will go a long way to increase the parent-child bond and to keep you in your child's focus on everything they do even though you are not physically there with them. Finally, intercede for them. Remember that prayer works. Prayer will keep your child safe in the hands of the Almighty God, who holds the future.

God Holds the Future

Often, young people are in a rush to leave home, but the God who holds the future is not in a hurry. He is already in the future and controls it. This world is loud and hurried, but God remains sovereign in it all. It is God who holds all the pieces together. Many young people have rushed forward without God and have been crushed. Do not rush and break; wait on God. He loves you, even in your weaknesses. He desires to guard you into a happy destiny. The question is, are you ready to walk humbly and patiently with him as you transition into adulthood?

A classic example of a young man who entrusted his future into God's hands was Joseph. At the tender age of seventeen, his brothers sold him into an unknown future. He did not know what his fate was, despite the dreams of great achievements that he had had. His only option was to trust God. Joseph was careful and intentional about doing just that, and the faithful God did not disappoint him. It was God's presence that made all the difference in his life. In Genesis 39, the phrase, "the Lord was with Joseph" appears three times. Verse 21 says, "the Lord was with him; he showed him kindness and granted him favor in the eyes of the prison warden." Making God and His kingdom a priority is a prerequisite for success.

The fact that God was with Joseph didn't mean life was easy for him. We know that he found himself in prison and was also falsely accused. So, Joseph faced challenges. What this phrase means is that the Lord granted him grace and strength to overcome any difficulty that came his way. God gave him supernatural abilities and favor to be successful. Joseph, however, had to embrace some godly principles. He was a man who feared God, honored his parents, and loved his brothers, even though they hated him. In the same way, as you resolve to place God first and sort your differences with your parents, He will give you special abilities to help you stand out and succeed in a future where your parents might not be the immediate influencers of your life.

The Influencers in the Next Phase

Everyone has specific influencers at some point in time. These are people who carry the ability to determine the direction of one's life. In this context, we are not just referring to social media influencers who carry considerable sway, but also other people—friends, acquaintances, and family—who influence you one way or another. Your priority shouldn't be to follow people because they have 2 million followers on Instagram, or they have 1,000,000 subscribers on YouTube. Instead, you should seek godly influencers who will have a positive impact on your life. Many young people have fallen prey to the wrong influencers with dire consequences. Others have also had their future beautifully shaped by connecting with the right influencers. Influencers determine your decisions and choices; choose wisely.

Young people continue to seek mentors and role models, as they go through the various stages in life. Your parents and immediate family may have played a critical role in influencing your values and beliefs all through your formative years—the people you spend time with the most shape most of your worldviews. A 1997 study conducted by researchers at the University of Minnesota and the University of North Carolina surveyed 12,000 students in grades 7 through 12. They found teenagers who are close to their parents are less likely to smoke, use drugs, drink alcohol, engage in violence, commit suicide, or have sex at a young age. [30] Several other studies have also found that most teens point to their parents as the most critical influence in their lives. Peers and media then follow.

Rice and Veerman identified the following primary influencers on teenagers:

- Parents
- Extended family
- Adults outside the home (teachers, coaches, youth workers)
- Same-age peers
- The media (TV, movies, music)[31]

As you transition to college or lead a somewhat independent life, you will realize that there might be a shift in your lineup of influencers. On your campus, or in the absence of parents and immediate family, peer groups, and social media could become your influencers. There are, however, several dangers in allowing social media to overly influence how you live your life. Many young people have fallen prey to bullies and predators on social media. Lori Getz, a social media expert, identified the following dangers to social media usage: "overfriending . . . overconnecting, and oversharing." *Overfriending* implies inviting someone to your online life whom you would not ask to your breakfast table. *Overconnecting* is communicating with multiple sites and applications, using the same username. You get lots of attention by doing this, but some attention can be distracting and unhelpful. It can also make you vulnerable in many ways. *Oversharing* is excessiveness in social media postings and sharing things such as your next trip to Las Vegas and indicating your location to the world at your every turn. In the absence of parental shelter, exposure to social media can open a new arena of danger to you.

Influencers can shape people's worldviews. These worldviews are what they are; they influence the world. It is, therefore, very essential for you to be aware of them and the impact they can have on your life. For instance, several young ladies have Oprah Winfrey as their influencer. Her general spirituality and New Age movement stance have confused many of her followers who have taken the position of "if I think it is right, then it might as well be right." Such anti-Christian worldviews can potentially dilute your pristine Christian view. Other worldviews, such as humanism, naturalism, Islamism, and postmodernism, can further complicate your ability to remain

As a young Christian, you don't have to consume everything that looks religious.

focused and to maintain your Christian values. As a young Christian, you don't have to consume everything that looks religious. Guard your faith in Christ with all the energy and attention that it deserves.

139

Contending for your faith requires that you surround yourself with Christians who carry similar biblical values like yourself. Even though it is okay to associate with people who don't share the same faith as you, you may need to ensure that those in your inner circle have some spiritual connection to your faith. If you associate with friends who take delight in going to the club and partying, you are likely to do the same. This season is the time to make some personal commitments to godly values and spiritual disciplines. These would become the pillars that would sustain you on campus and beyond.

Every single person in scripture who accomplished something worthwhile had to fight for what they believed. People like Daniel, Joseph, Esther, and Paul the apostle had to fight against the tide. It did cost them rejection and suffering. However, it brought them lots of reward. Quoting from a hymnal by Horatius Bonar, "Go Labor On" a line reads "Men heed thee, love thee, praise thee not; The Master praises: what are men?" We advise that don't try to fit in on campus, in your community or wherever you may find yourself. Know who you are; you are a unique being with clearly defined mandate. Your goal is to fulfill this God-given mandate, rather than seeking to please men.

Faith and the Pressure on Campus

College students go through significant transitions. They deal with a lot of pressure. It is the stage when most people gain their independence and fend for themselves. The pressure on the minds of students can be overwhelming. Recently, one college Christian campus president invited us to their revival night program. This program focused on emotional and mental healing. She told us: *"Many of the students on my campus admit they developed a mental problem when they came to live on campus. Depression and heaviness are real right here on our campus. And a lot of people are struggling."*

College students use different strategies to deal with their stresses. Some may choose to associate with various groups, which could range from a few friends, small groups, to clubs. Such associations may either have a positive or negative influence on them. However, since most college students are naïve and desperate to belong, they may join groups without even knowing the consequences. Some of these groups may look harmless on the surface. They could present themselves as support groups, which make several promises of helping their members succeed academically and in their careers. However, for some of these clubs, at the back end of these promises are rituals and rites of passages that may require a renunciation of faith in God.

Some of these campus organizations emphasize the use of "brother" and "sister" to signify their unity. However, they bind members in commitments and lifestyles that may be extremely detrimental to their faith in Christ. As part of activities, students go through bizarre experiences such as hair shaving, foul confessions, abuses, immoral activities, and heavy drinking, among others. Often, these students join without knowing the spiritual and ethical implications. As a

Any organization that has beliefs contrary to your Christian faith should be off your list.

Christian student, you must be careful what you sign on to—don't join a club because you want to fit in. Instead, ensure that before you decide to join any association, you must research what they stand for. Any organization that has beliefs contrary to your Christian faith should be off your list. It is true these clubs can support you in so many ways. But, where does all that support come from? God is the one that can supply all your needs according to his riches in glory (Phil. 4:19). If you trust him, he will make a way for you, and do more than what man can promise you, without you bending any scriptural principles.

Instead of joining these groups for belongingness and support, we encourage you to consider joining a good Christian group among the several Bible-based organizations on campus. Organizations such as the Pentecost Students and Associates, Campus Crusade for Christ, A-Life, InterVarsity Christian Fellowship, and others are good organizations to belong to for fellowship and support. If none align with your beliefs, you can start something new.

Wherever you find yourself, don't forget you are a Christian first. Hence, it is essential to maintain your godly principles and any cultural values that may have positively shaped you. As you transition from home, and increasingly gain your independence, you will realize that the training you received from your parents was not all irrelevant and burdening. You may still not like their approach to bringing you up because of your cultural differences. However, those values and lessons would prove to you that, even though you and your parents are years apart, your cultural values are quite similar.

CHAPTER EIGHT

WE ARE NOT SO DIFFERENT AFTER ALL

Having somewhere to go is home. Having someone to love is family. Having both is a blessing —Unknown

"Mom, I honestly wish you were my mom" *[chuckles].*

"Yes, Martha. I am. I am your spiritual mom."

"Not like that. I mean, I wish you were my biological mom, and, like, I am living with you."

"Oh, okay. I get it now. Why do you say so?"

"Because I like the way you treat and interact with your girls. Anytime I visit, I observe a lot, and I realize that even when they do something bad, and you chastise them, you follow it with hugs and kisses. And besides, I like the way you relate to all of us girls. You seem so understanding. I know you are strict—"

[laughs]

"—but you are never judgmental, and that makes it easy for us to come to you with any issues bothering us."

"Aw, thanks for the kind words. Well, this didn't happen in a day. We [Pastor (this is George) and I] both grew up in Ghana and adopted certain aspects of African parenting. Believe it or not, we used the parental knowledge that we learned from our parents on the kids, because that is all we knew. I remember when our first child was a toddler, we would punish her at the least provocation. I [Cynthia] remember I taught her to say 'sorry' before she could barely talk, and she would often say, 'wawwy, mommy' [chuckles], looking miserable. The standards and expectations we had for her were way above her age level. When she turned four, we realized she began seeing the unnecessary restrictions as hate. That is when we bought our first parenting book: "Spiritually Parenting Your Preschooler: Start Your Children on the Right Path to Know God" by C. Hope Flinchbaugh. We read it together as a couple, and honestly, it was the beginning of our unlearning specific parenting styles and learning new methods."

"Wow! I wish my mom had read that book too, or would at least see the point in reading it. I am sure she would have yelled at me and beaten me less." [laughs]

"Well, it's not too late. That is why we are sounding the siren and letting all immigrant parents and children alike know that there are better ways of relating to each other. And one thing the younger generation should refrain from is playing the blame game. Rather, you should strive to meet your parents in a middle way. Parents are just using skills they were taught or saw growing up. Trust me, most parents do not mean evil. The cultures are simply different. If the youth will cultivate *that understanding, and parents would be willing to adjust to their culture, the home will be more peaceful."*

"But Mommy, our parents think they are always right and are not ready to listen to anything we say."

"I can imagine. But, have you thought about the approach you use to addressing these issues? African parents demand respect. So, you must be cautious and wise when you are addressing issues like these with them. Sometimes, you guys just assume they are all wrong and irrelevant, and if you take that approach, they won't listen to you."

"Mommy, you don't understand. They just don't get it!"

"Yeah, I agree, and you don't get it either." [both laugh] "See how you are pushing all the blame on your parents. The only way to solve this generational or cultural problem is to admit that each generation is unique and different, and either generation has to embrace these differences and find common grounds for coexistence."

"I guess you prevailed over me." [chuckles] "I understand. My mom has been mean, but I know I haven't been that great either."

Some of the girls at our church came home to visit. As we sat down over drinks and cookies, we discussed various issues bothering them. Earlier on, I (Cynthia) had asked one of our daughters to get something for me. While the girls were still around, I called her and asked about my request, and she apologized because she had forgotten, and instead, she went to her room. I wasn't happy about it, but I patiently rebuked her, and hugged her, after which I asked her to attend to that request. Martha, one of the girls who had visited, observed our interactions. After my daughter left, she engaged me in the above conversation. My interaction with Martha points to the realities of the parent-child relationship in most African immigrant homes. It also highlights the youth's preference for culturally tolerant environments than an environment that is imposing and harsh.

Most African immigrant parents perceive themselves as "Africans first and members of a national group second."[32] Even though these parents seem to have effectively submerged themselves in Western economies, particularly the job markets, they haven't embraced Western culture to the same extent. A survey by Bloomberg's Justin Fox revealed that African nationals from Ghana, Kenya, Ethiopia, and Nigeria are the most hard-working people in the United States.[33] They are also

This finding suggests that first-generation immigrant parents may have embraced the Western economic culture, but not much of its values and beliefs.

some of the most educated. This finding suggests that first-generation immigrant parents may have embraced the Western economic culture, but not much of its values and beliefs. They see Western cultural ideals as individualistic, undisciplined, materialistic, and violent.[34]

Similarly, most children of such immigrant parents, even those born in America, usually identify themselves with their parents' culture, regardless of whether they get along with them or not. For most of the youth, there is a dual pride and a dual cultural heritage.[35] Like their immigrant parents, the youth seldom approve of insubordinate attitudes of children towards their parents in the mainstream culture, and they strive for a sense of community.

However, they seek for a bit of personal space and respect as well, values that are prevalent in Western culture. Here, we are not saying that Western culture doesn't uphold such values on respect and honor. What we stress is that due to the more liberal cultural stance of Western culture, if a child swerves from doing the right thing, the corrective measures may not be strong deterrents. In our focus group discussion, Abigail narrated an incident that occurred while her friend's mother dropped her at her house after a play date. On the way, her friend Brittany started cussing. When her mother asked her to stop, Brittany got furious and told her:

> *"Shut up, mom. You are so annoying. Just leave me alone. The next time you tell me what to do, I am going to get out of this car."*

Abigail attempted to correct Brittany by telling her that it was not okay to talk to her mother like that. Brittany responded:

> *"She always gets into my business. I don't like it when she gets into my business when I am with my friends."*

Even though such attitudes are unacceptable in most cultures, in the African culture, a child dares not speak to their parents in this manner. The young and old alike understand these values, and both groups are proud of their African heritage that upholds respect for the elderly and the exhibition of proper manners. The question then is, why is there so much tension in African homes, homes with people who are "Africans at heart" and with similar cultural values?

What each generational group fails to acknowledge is that opinions may differ, attitudes may be worlds apart, choices may be as vast as the sea, and traits may vary drastically between the two, but their core values remain the same. The two groups may not necessarily appreciate their differences. Nonetheless, the only way they can peacefully live together is if they mutually understand themselves. But they cannot understand each other if they don't fully know themselves. Knowing each other requires that they step into their respective worlds, even though it might look foreign. Such a perspective will help to appreciate each other's opinions and struggles better and enable the immigrant family to value the other person enough not to let differing opinions destroy their bond.

Immigrant parents and their children may think differently and disagree on issues, but they are the same family. Mom might like *eba* and *egusi* stew, and Ngozi might prefer *egusi* stew with chicken wings and fried potatoes. Likewise, Ama may prefer eating *jollof* rice but will not have anything to do with *fufu*. It's okay for a child to be assertive to a certain extent. However, if an immigrant child is taking certain decisions that may harm his or her life, especially with regards to friends, relationships, and careers, parental intervention would be necessary. It would not be helpful for the child to ignore the parents' concern in the name of being in a different generation or culture. Neither is it always okay for parents to impose their will on their children. If a mutual relationship exists between parents and their children, the two parties can use sincere and honest

What each generational group fails to acknowledge is that opinions may differ, attitudes may be worlds apart, choices may be as vast as the sea, and traits may vary drastically between the two, but their core values remain the same.

conversations to resolve any conflict and misunderstandings that may arise between them.

For proper consensus building between youth and their parents, they should strive to negotiate or compromise on specific grounds. We enrolled our first child in gymnastics when she was four years old. The only reason we did that was that she used to take dance classes, not because we saw that talent in her, but at that stage, we were trying to figure out her passion and abilities. She came home one day, at the age of five, and said to us, "I like the music at the dance school better than the music at church." The hip-hop class came right after her class. So, she was referring to the secular hip-hop music beats. This issue may sound funny, but we felt as Christian parents, we had to rethink our decision to expose her to something that was taking the place of what was supposed to be her first love—God. So, we decided to switch her over to gymnastics. She fell in love with gymnastics right away, and we realized she was great at it; every misfortune is a blessing in disguise indeed.

We bring this story up because the extracurricular activity we randomly enrolled our child in turned into a talent that we could barely manage. Unexpectedly, something that was for fun ended up as a passionate pursuit, which at some point, she was prioritizing over her studies. In response, we pulled her out of gymnastics for a year so she could focus on her education. She was unhappy. Within that period, she self-taught and did not miss much of the skills she was supposed to learn at practice. Although we tried, we could not prevent her from pursuing her passion. At that point, we realized we couldn't just impose our wishes on her. We dialogued with her, but with a caveat. She could go back to gymnastics so long as it didn't hurt her education. We explained to her that there was no guarantee that she could easily make a sustainable career from gymnastics in the future. We advised her to prioritize her education, and she did. She went back to the gym, maintained a straight

A status in middle school, and did nine hours a week of gymnastics. It was a win-win situation: the parents win, the child wins.

It's a Different Era

Immigrant parents struggle to cope in a different environment. Likewise, their children do not find it comfortable maneuvering between multiple cultures. Both parents and children can find a reasonable approach to negotiate between their complex cultural worlds. One way to do so is for parents to help their children effectively adapt to the African culture by continually exposing them to it in a more tolerable and understandable way. They can do this by either taking them on holiday to their home country to experience their culture or create opportunities for them to associate with peers of similar backgrounds. Parents can also narrate the histories of their lands, family backgrounds, people, childhood, and church gatherings growing up.

Daily interactions in the home can convey some of the cultural values parents seek to pass on to their children. Parents should also let their children know they embrace the positive aspects of Western culture. Doing this will ensure that while they immerse them in Western culture, they are consistently exposing these children to the African culture.

The cultural approach we suggest in this book is similar to the thoughts Gary Chapman shares in his book *The 5 Love Languages: The Secret to Love that Lasts.*[36] He highlights that to express love adequately, the giver should communicate it in a way that the recipient understands. He further explains that even though parents love their teens, "thousands of teens do not feel that love. For most parents, it is not a matter of sincerity, but rather lack of information on how to communicate love effectively on an emotional level." Gary highlights in all his love language series that there are five love languages: words of affirmation, physical touch, quality time, acts of service, and gifts—for each person, one language dominates. The most effective way to communicate love to someone is when you speak the language they understand—their love language. In other words, context matters. In line with Chapman's idea, immigrant parents can improve communication with their children if they situate such interaction within the cultural setting where they raise these children. That way, they can pass on their cultural values in a way these children understand. Onwujuba and Marks cite instances of African and Asian immigrant parents' approach to balancing their heritage culture and the American culture.[37] They explain how, with time, immigrant parents might decide to change their premigration parenting practices in favor of more of the American style of parenting. In their study, they revealed that first-generation Korean parents uphold their strict parenting values. However, in adjusting to Western culture, they have gradually moved away from spanking and increased their show of affection in their disciplinary measures.[38] This approach does not necessarily condone the excessive freedoms in decision-making and over-praising children for insignificant achievements, which are dominant features in Western culture. Instead, it borrows from the more humane and collaborative approach to discipline from the Western context, where parents explain why they are disciplining the child.

In line with Chapman's idea, immigrant parents can improve communication with their children if they situate such interaction within the cultural setting where they raise these children.

Such a path is likely to produce a more positive outcome than spanking and yelling, which may be carried out without explanation:

> *Some of the cultural differences that result in conflict between my parents and I, in general, is the misunderstanding in everything. They always yell and scream and insult you, and you don't even know why they are yelling. So, I can't go to them for anything or talk to them apart from if I need something.*

—*Gabby, fourteen years old*

Disciplining out of emotions amounts to punishment. To be effective at parenting, we suggest that African immigrant parents should pay attention to the difference between punishment and discipline.[39] Punishment suggests repaying someone with what they deserve. The goal of every parent is to train their children to be responsible. It is never to repay them for their wrongdoings. However, the approach most immigrant parents use to correct their children may come across as punishment.

In several immigrant homes, parents focus on reminding their children of their repeated offenses, and they express their frustrations through yelling and name-calling. The results of such actions on their children include fear, guilt, timidity, hatred, and low self-image. Immigrant parents may need to change the focus and attitude of their disciplinary measures if they want to see positive results. Ingram suggests that as a parent, if you are so angry at your child,

Experiential knowledge means they must see things from each other's perspectives rather than acting on assumptions on what they think constitutes the other's culture.

"there's nothing wrong with taking time to invite God to "clothe" you in the Spirit of Christ, remind yourself that Jesus has already paid for your children's sins, ask God to help you handle your anger appropriately, and then deal with the situation rationally."[40]

Parents who feel liberalism in Western culture makes it difficult for them to assert their authority on their children can sometimes act radically. These parents could decide to send their children to their home countries. While such a decision may prove beneficial, in some cases, it could leave a lot of psychological and emotional scars on children. The parental separation and having to adjust to a culture that is vastly different from their own can be daunting for them. Others may be abused physically, emotionally, and sexually by family members or close acquaintances who may take advantage of the situation. If this should happen, the complexities in such family dynamics could make the victims afraid to share with their parents, resulting in a lot of emotional instability.

> *As both worlds strive to converge, they will realize that their goals are the same, but the meanings and methods of achieving them may differ.*

If immigrant parents can understand their children and reasonably relate with them, and their children will listen and appreciate them, such drastic actions may not be necessary. As a parent, if you must send your child back to your country at all costs, you should carefully weigh your decision before taking this step.

The Need for Convergence

For peaceful coexistence to occur, immigrant parents and their children would have to meet each other in a middle way. One way to achieve a middle way is to strive to know each other through experiential learning, rather than assumed knowledge. Experiential knowledge means they must see things from each other's perspectives rather than acting on assumptions on what they think constitutes the other's culture. If parents explore the culture of their children, they will realize that these young ones are as ambitious as they are towards life goals and cultural values. Parents' perception of a good future—which is a meaningful and fulfilling life—is similar to that of their children. However, what constitutes a fulfilled life for the older generation may mean something different for the younger generation. As both worlds strive to converge, they will realize that their goals are the same, but the meanings and methods of achieving them may differ. That is where the conflict lies.

Youthful life can be overly ambitious and unrealistic at the same-time. For many young people, youthful exuberance has a minimal basis. So, even though most young people strive to be the best they can, their approach may lack experience. Parents face the challenge of patiently dealing with a generation that is enthusiastic and talented but needs additional knowledge to develop their potentials fully. The parent should, therefore, serve as the conduit through which the right experience and direction can flow to the child.

Young people live in a complicated world with many voices and signposts. Mueller equates this to a first timer in Time Square, New York. This newbie may know where he is going but may be unsure about the direction to take. So, he chooses to follow the loudest noise and the most attractive and convincing signposts[41]. This choice is easier if friends or peers are following it as well. The loudest voices are the voices that seem authentic, understanding, and convincing, without sounding pushy. Like the Time Square newbie, youth of today face such a dilemma. Amid multiple voices and signposts, where should they turn?

There is a hidden lesson for parents from the above analogy. The average youth has a purpose but may lack a sense of direction. To attract their attention and guide them on the right path, parents must adopt strategies that are appealing, convincing, and not pushy. We counseled an exceptionally talented young lady, Mabel, who had a passion for the arts. She had to change her major in the arts and pursue a career in business, based on her parents' preference. As we spoke to her, we realized the dissatisfaction about the new route she was taking, so we advised her to pursue her talent on the side. What baffled us was the fact that we discovered she was trying different things, besides her main career goal, and her passion in the arts. As we spent more time with her, we observed she felt the need to do something or launch something out there to carve a niche. She saw several of her peers doing different things on social media, and she felt she should do the same. The new opportunities she was trying to pursue were adding more stress to her already packed college life. We saw passion and purpose in Mabel, but we also observed a lack of direction.

Some lessons emerge from Mabel's story. First, her immigrant parents want the best for her and believe a career in the arts may not bring her enough income. Her parents may have this mentality due to their knowledge of which jobs sell. From what they know, a career in business or the sciences can produce a more stable income than those in the arts. So, here the parents had good intentions for Mabel. However, they lacked all the information to make this decision but know from experience that poor career choices can be disastrous in the future. On the other hand, Mabel has read about her arts field and seen people in America succeed in the same career that she originally planned to pursue. Hence, she couldn't understand the reason behind her parents' disapproval. Mabel agreed to drop her previous major only to please them. She sincerely believed she could make a living in the arts, but then what are the guarantees? She did not think about that.

In the story of Mabel and her parents, she had "the knowledge" while her parents had "the experience." Her parents may be right or wrong, and the same applies to Mabel since each side doesn't possess the full information. Because children are more immersed in the mainstream culture, they may have more knowledge on specific issues than their immigrant parents. Likewise, parents have understanding and wisdom due to their maturity and experience, as highlighted in the book of Job: "Is not wisdom found among the aged? Does not long life bring understanding?" (Job 12:12). It is in such instances that parents and their children can cooperatively combine their knowledge and experience to provide a better solution to such dilemmas. In Mabel's case, proper dialoguing, parental experience, and Mabel's knowledge would have resulted in a more amicable solution. It would have also prevented Mabel from seeking any other pursuits, which could potentially derail her career ambitions altogether.

A lack of understanding between parents and their young ones can have negative consequences on college choices, which may result in lost opportunities. Some parents disagree with their children on which college to select. Some youth may choose to go several hundreds of miles away from home for college or other reasons. Parents, who assume such children are going away because they want to be free to do their own thing, may oppose such a move. In certain instances, specific colleges could offer better opportunities for these children. Michael narrated his frustration when he was preparing for college:

> *I was this close to going to Columbia University but an argument with my dad about the distance from home shut it all down because he wouldn't even wait to listen to what I had*

to say. He didn't realize we have a family in New York that would've been happy to help me live there at such a prestigious school. Failing to listen to me, as they always do, has shattered my dreams. I am so angry and so not happy at my current college.

—Michael, twenty years old

In the Western educational system, the transition from high school to college is a tricky one. For instance, engagement in extracurricular activities and knowledge of a foreign language can increase your competitive urge for acceptance and funding. Unfortunately, extracurricular activities are a significant area of contention for immigrant families because of financial obligations, time commitments, and the general belief that they are a waste of time.

Doing extracurricular activities in school is problematic for my dad because he thinks it's nonsense. However, it is likely to help me get into college, seeming like a well-rounded student in this day and age. Parents think it's all about grades, but it's much more than that to get into college.

—Emelia, seventeen years old

In some instances, parents may need to trust the knowledge of their children, who are more exposed to such opportunities in the mainstream culture through their school and extensive social networks. In such pursuits, parents may nonetheless need to guide children in their decision-making. Immigrant parents must realize that the mainstream culture is different, and what it takes to succeed differs from the culture they know. The only way you and your children can successfully maneuver through this sophisticated culture is through mutual learning, understanding, and consensus building.

Compromise: A Mindset Shift

Immigrant families can win their war in their homes if both parents and children are willing to drop their cultural weapons. That means stepping out of each other's comfort zone and adopting the ethical aspects of their respective cultures. Most of the African immigrant parents we interviewed fall within the age category of the Generation X population in the American context, which is between forty-one and fifty-four years. However, due to the predominantly African cultural mindset, they are raising their Millennial and Generation Z kids with parenting styles and ideals of generations much older than them. Immigrant parents would need to step out of their cultural world and embrace a Millennial/Generation Z world. The young Millennials and Generation Z'ers will also have to meet their parents in a middle way. Both groups must merge their cultures into a blend from which they can all drink. We call this a "cultural compromise"—which is a blended culture, comprising a bit of the African and a bit of the Western culture. This cultural mix, which has multiple flavors, may not necessarily be sweet. However, the fact that it has some familiar flavor should make it acceptable to both worlds.

Immigrant families can win their war in their homes if both parents and children are willing to drop their cultural weapons.

As a parent who may hold different values and beliefs from the Western culture, understanding the culture does not necessarily mean you agree with it or adopt it entirely. What that means is you are trying to understand your Western-born or raised child, who is heavily influenced by that culture. Distancing yourself from the mainstream culture does not mean you can escape its impact on you and your child. If something significantly affects your child, it makes sense to figure out what it entails. Therefore, we encourage all parents to take a step back and assess how you have related to your child. Such a reflection will help you determine the necessary adjustments to make in relating to your child. This change will require that you let go of some upheld values and allow your child a little room to operate. It will also require that you facilitate open communication with them.

Immigrant parents should strive to adjust their relationship dynamics, and their children must appreciate their effort. As a young person, you may find it awkward to kiss your mother. Still, if she at least tries to hug you, which may be a more comfortable way to express affection, this can extend a show of love. Your father may not be fluent in English, but know that he is the only dad you have. He may not be fluent in English, but he is fluent in his local dialect. Several Asian and South American parents can barely speak English. So, the lack of fluency is not unique to the African immigrant culture. We are not advocating complacency and refusal of parents to learn English in the

This cultural mix, which has multiple flavors, may not necessarily be sweet. However, the fact that it has some familiar flavor should make it acceptable to both worlds.

mainstream culture. What we stress here is for youth to know that just as it isn't their fault that they were born or raised in the West, in the same way, it is not the fault of their parents either that they are not fluent in English. So, they must tolerate and respect them, regardless of who and how they are. For instance, they may not fit the ideal Western parent. However, know that they possess values, wisdom, and a wealth of experience that can benefit you.

In our home, we have family times with our three children. Often, we play silly games, and once a while, we may pronounce a word or say something (trying to be relevant to them) in a way that they would tell us jokingly that it sounds funny. However, they don't say it in a mean way, and we all have a big laugh over it. The immigrant family may be different, culturally. Still, you should all strive to live peacefully with each other, and celebrate your differences instead of allowing them to divide you.

For some children raised in immigrant homes, your parents may come across as a bit too strict, or you may feel the house chores are way too much. If you think your parents are overly protective or unrealistic, you should talk to them patiently and help them understand what you think. The key to their receptiveness is your attitude and approach. Sometimes when you don't get a yes, you should obey them. Your parents want the best for you. Once you know that they mean well, it is easier to embrace their rules and directives, which, of course, should not be an imposition, but an engagement. For the most part, you may not know the benefits of all that your parents are doing until you leave home when the life lessons that they instilled in you become handy.

Some youth may be upset when their parents make a big deal about providing for them and using that as a reason for them to want them to be more responsible. But know that nurturing is a difficult job. Maybe, the way your parents express themselves in such instances doesn't make sense to you. You may feel all they care about is taking care of your physical needs and not so much of your emotional and other needs. But as a young one reading this book, we encourage you to take a step back and appreciate them for taking care of you, rather than trivializing what they do. Such appreciations would open the door for discussing the other needs you may have.

Discipline is a big topic in the African immigrant home. We encourage parents to use the nonabusive methods of training. But on the part of the youth, it might be helpful to refrain from adopting the aspects of Western culture that your parents may completely disagree with. For instance, talking back is not a common thing in African culture. Therefore, even though you may desire a listening ear, restrain yourselves from the tendency to talk back. Instead, you can find a good time to talk to your parents.

The bottom line is both parents and their children must be willing to adjust their cultural mindset towards each other. Remember that it takes two to tango, and at the same time, it takes two to make things right.

FINAL THOUGHTS

The African culture is terrific; so is the Western culture. However, both cultures have their flaws. Immigrant families who face multiple cultures and identities must find a way to blend the two cultures if they are to live peacefully. Parents must know that besides their African culture, their children need Western culture to be relevant in that environment. Besides, this culture is required to be successful in school and be competitive in the workplace. For instance, self-confidence is a profound trait among young people. An immigrant parent who supports the virtues of humility and self-control may easily take the self-confident demeanor of their child to mean arrogance. But young people need a certain level of self-confidence to survive in Western culture.

It is instead a conflict arising from two worlds—worlds that are not so different in values but far apart in approaches.

In the same way, the youth should understand that their parents are Africans first. They can never change to take on another culture entirely. The African culture is beautiful; it is the excessive components that may not be so helpful. So, young people must allow their parents to be Africans, and they must be proud of it, just like the Asians and Latinos are. What they can do is assist their parents in learning the ethical components of Western culture, which will improve their relationships, and ease their transition into that culture.

When immigrant parents and their children find common grounds of coexistence by seeing things from each other's perspective, they will realize that their disagreement is not because of sheer hatred for each other. Neither is it because of contempt for each other's culture. It is instead a conflict arising from *two worlds*—worlds that are not so different in values but far apart in approaches. The only way to marry both worlds is to highlight the shared values and find common grounds of collaboration to reduce the cultural conflict between both worlds.

The need to resolve these conflicts is why we wrote: *Two Worlds at War: Finding Common Cultural Grounds for African Immigrant Parents and their Children.* In this book, we took the reader into the home of the African immigrant family to see firsthand the differences in both worlds. Paul admonishes in 1 Corinthians 1:10: "I appeal to you, brothers and sisters, in the name of our Lord Jesus Christ, that all of you agree with one another in what you say and that there be no divisions among you, but that you be perfectly united in mind and thought." We believe that the cultural tension in immigrant homes resulting from different generations and cultures should not necessarily result in a war. Instead, families should use such diversity to develop healthy relationships in their homes. That way, they can build homes that are not warring but winning.

NOTES

ENDNOTES

1   Oparaoji, M. N. (2015). *Raising an African child in America-from the perspective of an immigrant Nigerian mom.* Xlibris: Indiana.

2   Ibid.

3   Shaw, H. (2015) *Generational IQ: Christianity isn't dying, millennials aren't the problem, and the future is bright.* Tyndale Momentum: Carol Stream, IL. Shaw categorizes the generations into: Traditionalists (before 1945); Baby Boomers (1945–1964); Generation X (1965–1980); and Millennials (1981–2001). He adds a "new generation" group, Generation Z for those born from 2002 and beyond, who are children of Generation X and the first half of the Millennial generation.

4   The Baby Boomers are those who are currently between 56–75 years, whereas Generation Xers fall within 40–55 years. For the most part, the younger Baby Boomers and Generation Xers have raised the millennial who are anywhere between 19–39 years, and Generation Xers and millennials are raising Generation Zers (who are 18 years and below). If you are a college student, you are likely to have a parent who falls within the category of Generation X, unless your parents had an early or late birth. On the other hand, a 35-year old professional would likely have either a Generation Xer or Baby Boomer parent. The children of the Millennials, Generation Z, are either in high school or below. Since we focus on youth ages 13 and 20, the parent group of interest to us is Generation X and their youth children who fall within the (younger) Millennial and Z Generations.

5   Huffington Post. Generation X's parenting problem. By Anjali
     Enjeti. May, 13th 2015.

6   Ibid.

7   Shaw, H. (2015) *Generational IQ: Christianity isn't dying, millen-
     nials aren't the problem, and the future is bright.* Tyndale Momentum:
     Carol Stream, IL.

8   Ibid

9   Yang, L. and Cash, M. 54 before-and-after photos that show
     how much the world has changed. Lucy Yang and Meredith
     Cash. Insider. May 16, 2019.

10   According to the U.S government the first member of a family
     to acquire citizenship or permanent resident status qualifies as
     the family's first generation. The U. S. Census Bureau defines
     only foreign-born individuals as first generation. Birth in the
     United States is therefore not a requirement, as first-genera-
     tion immigrants may be either foreign-born residents or U.S.-
     born children of immigrants, depending on who you ask. For
     this study, we consider foreign-born immigrants as first-genera-
     tion immigrants and their American raised or born children as
     second-generation immigrants. The children born in America,
     however, are also considered as first-generation American-born.

11   This is acculturation into the host culture. Acculturation is
     assimilation to a different culture, typically the dominant one.
     Research has shown that immigrant children acculturate into
     a dominant culture at a rate much faster than their parents
     because the former are in their formative years.

12   Szapocznik, J., & Williams, R. A. (2000). Brief strategic family
     therapy: Twenty-five years of interplay among theory, research
     and practice in adolescent behavior problems and drug abuse.
     [Review]. *Clinical Child and Family Psychology Review*, 3(2), 117–134.

13   Thiong'o, N. (1994). Decolonizing the mind: The politics of lan-
     guage in African literature. East African Educational Publishers.

14 Rice, W. & Veerman D. (1999). *Understanding your teenager*. Word Publishing, Nashville, TN.

15 Hemmen, L. (2012). *Parenting a teen girl: A crash course on conflict, communication & connection with your teenage daughter*. New Harbinger Publications, Inc. Oakland, CA.

16 Onyinah, O., & Annor, G. (2016). *Myth or mystery: A bio-autobiography of Apostle Professor Opoku Onyinah*. Inved (UK).

17 Wolf, A. E. W. (2011). *I'd listen to my parents if they'd just shut up: What to say and not say when parenting teens*. Harper Collins Publishers: New York: NY

18 Thefreedictionary.com

19 Dale Carnegie (1998). *How to win friends and influence people*. New York: Gallery.

20 Onwujuba, C. and Mark, L. (2015). Why we do what we do: Reflections of educated Nigerian immigrants on their changing parenting attitudes and practices. *Family Science Review* 30(2) 23- 46.

21 There are four main types of parenting: authoritative, authoritarian, permissive, and uninvolved. Authoritative parenting communicates and explains household rules to the child in a respectful and warm, but firm, tone. With authoritarian parenting, the child is expected to follow the strict rules established by parents. Permissive parents allow freedom with little or no responsibility, and uninvolved parenting is characterized by low responsiveness and little communication. (http://theattached-family.com/membersonly/?p=2151).

22 Wolf, A. E. W. (2011). *I'd listen to my parents if they'd just shut up: What to say and not say when parenting teens*. Harper Collins Publishers: New York: NY.

23 Onwujuba, C. and Mark, L. (2015). Why we do what we do: Reflections of educated Nigerian immigrants on their

changing parenting attitudes and practices. *Family Science Review* 30(2) 23- 46.

24 The Pew Research Center. Generations apart—and together. August 12 2009. https://www.pewsocialtrends. org/2009/08/12/ii-generations-apart-and-together/

25 Ali, M., and K. Kilbride. 2004. Forging New Ties: Improving parenting and family support services for New Canadians with young children. Ottawa: Human Resources and Skills Development, Canada.

26 Ibid.

27 Kinnaman, D. (2011). *You lost me*. Baker Books. Grand Rapids, MI.

28 Koduah, A. (2019). Managing the decline of Christianity in the Western World: Lessons for Churches in the developing world. Quarterfold Printabilities; Mumbai: India.

29 Agyemang-Amoako, M. (2019). Is he my father's God or my own God?—Apologetics for children. Volume 1.

30 Rice, W. & Veerman D. (1999). *Understanding your teenager*. Word Publishing, Nashville, TN.

31 Ibid.

32 In Motion: The African American migration experience. The Schomburg Center for Research in Black Culture, New York. [exhibit] April 2006, p. 8.

33 Fox, J., Wanted educated immigrants? Let in more Africans-highly skilled? Check. Hardworking? Check. English-speaking? Check. Ready to integrate? Check. Politics & Policy. Blomberg: March 16th, 2018.

34 In Motion: The African American migration experience. The Schomburg Center for Research in Black Culture, New York. [exhibit] April 2006.

35 Usher, K. (2004, February 25) 2nd generation immigrants from Africa have dual pride. Chicago Tribune. Retrieved from https://www.chicagotribune.com/news/ct-xpm-2004–02–25–0402250115-story.html

36 Chapman, G. (2014). *The Five Love Languages: The Secret to Love that Lasts.* Northfield Publishing, Chicago, IL.

37 Onwujuba, C. and Mark, L. (2015). Why we do what we do: Reflections of educated Nigerian immigrants on their changing parenting attitudes and practices. *Family Science Review* 30(2) 23- 46.

38 Kim, E. & Hong, S. (2007). First-generation Korean American parents' perceptions of discipline. *Journal of Professional Nursing,* 23(1), 60–68.

39 Ingram, C. (2006). Punishment versus discipline. Focus on the Family. Accessed: https://www.focusonthefamily.com/parenting/effective-biblical-discipline/effective-child-discipline/punishment-versus-discipline. Taken from: *Effective Parenting in a Defective World.* Tyndale House Publishers, Inc.

40 Ibid

41 Mueller, W. (2006). *Engaging the soul of the youth culture: Bridging teen worldviews and Christian truth.* InterVarsity Press. Downers Grove: IL.